Physical Education for Students With Autism Spectrum Disorders

A Comprehensive Approach

Physical Education for Students With Autism Spectrum Disorders

A Comprehensive Approach

Michelle Grenier, PhD

University of New Hampshire

Editor

Human Kinetics

Library of Congress Cataloging-in-Publication Data

Physical education for students with autism spectrum disorders : comprehensive approach / Michelle Grenier, Editor.
  pages cm
 Includes bibliographical references and index.
 1. Physical education for children with disabilities. 2. Autism spectrum disorders. I. Grenier, Michelle, 1956-
 GV445.P52 2013
 371.9'04486--dc23

                                   2013002877

 ISBN-10: 1-4504-1973-9 (print)
 ISBN-13: 978-1-4504-1973-4 (print)

The web addresses cited in this text were current as of May 2013, unless otherwise noted.

Acquisitions Editor: Cheri Scott; **Developmental Editor:** Melissa Feld; **Assistant Editor:** Rachel Fowler; **Copyeditor:** Patsy Fortney; **Indexer:** Dan Connolly; **Permissions Manager:** Dalene Reeder; **Graphic Designer:** Nancy Rasmus; **Graphic Artist:** Dawn Sills; **Cover Designer:** Keith Blomberg; **Photograph (cover):** © Michelle Grenier; **Photographs (interior):** Photos on pages 18, 26, 74, 75 (all photos), 76 (all photos), 77 (all photos), 78, 79, 80, 81, 82, 83 (all photos), 84 (all photos), 85 (all photos), 86 (top photo), 88, 89, 91, 92, 94 (all photos), 96, 100, 101, and 103 © Ann Griffin; photos on pages 5, 7, 31 (all photos), 116, 119, 121 (all photos), and 125 © Pat Yeaton; photos on pages 21 and 86 (bottom photo) © Human Kinetics; photo on page 22 courtesy of David Barnes, CMARS; photo on page 23 © BOLD STOCK / age fotostock; **Photo Asset Manager:** Laura Fitch; **Visual Production Assistant:** Joyce Brumfield; **Photo Production Manager:** Jason Allen; **Art Manager:** Kelly Hendren; **Associate Art Manager:** Alan L. Wilborn; **Illustrations:** © Human Kinetics, unless otherwise noted; **Printer:** United Graphics

Printed in the United States of America   10 9 8 7 6 5 4 3 2 1

The paper in this book is certified under a sustainable forestry program.

Human Kinetics
Website: www.HumanKinetics.com

United States: Human Kinetics
P.O. Box 5076
Champaign, IL 61825-5076
800-747-4457
e-mail: humank@hkusa.com

Canada: Human Kinetics
475 Devonshire Road Unit 100
Windsor, ON N8Y 2L5
800-465-7301 (in Canada only)
e-mail: info@hkcanada.com

Europe: Human Kinetics
107 Bradford Road
Stanningley
Leeds LS28 6AT, United Kingdom
+44 (0) 113 255 5665
e-mail: hk@hkeurope.com

Australia: Human Kinetics
57A Price Avenue
Lower Mitcham, South Australia 5062
08 8372 0999
e-mail: info@hkaustralia.com

New Zealand: Human Kinetics
P.O. Box 80
Torrens Park, South Australia 5062
0800 222 062
e-mail: info@hknewzealand.com

E5586

...to my mother, Mimi; and my children, Martine, Lily, and Liam.

Contents

PART II   Individual and Small-Group Games and Activities

Preface

Current estimates are that one out of every 88 children born in the United States will have some form of autism (Autism Speaks, n.d.). The term *autism spectrum disorders* (ASD) includes the autistic disorder, Asperger syndrome, pervasive developmental disorder not otherwise specified (PDD-NOS), Rett syndrome, and child disintegrative disorder. However, with the new publication of the *Diagnostic and Statistical Manual of Mental Disorder* (DSM-5), all of the subcategories have merged under the umbrella of ASD. Other changes include the reduction of the three primary categories of ASD (social difficulties, communication impairments, and repetitive or restrictive behaviors) into two categories identified as social-communication impairment and repetitive or restrictive behaviors. Although many have strong cognitive skills, it is often the social and behavioral aspects of their personalities that pose the biggest challenges for teachers in physical education (PE). In turn, these aspects can affect skill acquisition and peer relationships, two key aspects of PE.

The Individuals with Disabilities Education Improvement Act (IDEIA) of 2005 continues to suggest inclusion in the general education classroom, including physical education, as the recommended practice for educating students with ASD. This is due to the social and academic gains that occur when these students are educated alongside their peers (Fisher & Meyer, 2002; Goodman & Williams, 2007; Schreibman, 2005). However ideal this may sound, in reality it can be a difficult process, particularly when PE teachers are given little additional support. This book is a how-to primer designed to give both adapted and general physical education teachers useful programming ideas for students with ASD.

The contributors of this book share a mutual interest in students with ASD as both researchers and practitioners. Our intention in writing this book was not to offer ways to "fix" or change students with ASD, but rather to give educators a number of options to consider when deciding how to work with their students. The methods of organizing instruction can be applied in general

and adapted physical education settings as well as alternative and recreational settings.

In our conversations with teachers, we have found that training and resources are foundational for a better understanding of their students with ASD. For the most part, teachers may have a general idea of the characteristics of ASD, but they don't always know how to deal with the specific behaviors when developing physical activity experiences. Questions teachers have include, Which instructional strategies should I use? What equipment works best? and, How do I know the student is making progress?

Oftentimes, students with ASD have trouble with social interactions and difficulty handling the loud, open space of the gymnasium. Group games can also be challenging for students with ASD who have poor motor skills and do not comprehend the social rules that involve sharing and taking turns. This book describes best practices from physical education, special education, and ASD training that will help practitioners meet their students' needs so they, too, can enjoy the benefits of physical activity. It introduces the inclusion spectrum as a tool for analyzing instruction to align students' abilities within the curriculum.

The primary contributors of this book are adapted and general physical education specialists whose collective experience spans decades of experience working with parents, special and general educators, and most important, students. Contributions from those in teacher education programs have also been solicited to discuss general research on the disability itself as well as assessment protocols that can be used to evaluate learning and the development of relevant individual education plan (IEP) goals and objectives.

Chapter 1, Understanding Students With Autism Spectrum Disorders, describes the characteristics of students on the autism spectrum and how their place on the spectrum affects learning. Chapter 2, Autism Spectrum Disorders From the Family Perspective, approaches ASD from both the parents' and teacher's perspective to gain insight into the challenges both face as well as potential strategies for working together. Chapter 3, Accessing the Curriculum Through the Inclusion Spectrum, offers a practical view on what can be done to meaningfully include students in physical education. Chapter 4, Proactive Strategies for Inclusion, describes the behaviors that affect learning and discusses the use of assistive technology, social stories, graphic organizers, and behavioral interventions in addressing these behaviors. Chapter 5, Reducing Stress to Optimize Learning, presents an overview of the stress response and its effect on learning in relation to people with ASD. Chapter 6, Assessment and the IEP Process, presents the challenges of assessing motor, physical fitness, and sport skill in children with ASD as well as ways to address those challenges, and explains how this information can be used to evaluate learning and develop relevant IEP goals and objectives. Chapter 7, Individualized Games and Activities, and chapter 8, Group Games and Activities, present lessons in the areas of motor and sport skill development, fitness, fundamental movement patterns, and perceptual motor skills for students from preschool through high school and beyond.

Each student with ASD is unique, and there is no one practice that will uniformly reach all students identified on the spectrum. Moreover, what works magically one day with a student may need to be reexamined the following day. Although being familiar with the characteristics of ASD helps to inform instruction, to develop a practice that reaches students, teachers need to consider the students themselves, what they are teaching, and the environment in which they are teaching. Individualizing instruction, in whatever context, is key. As Ann Griffin, one of our contributors, states, "When you get it right for this group of students, you will also have it right for all of the other students you are teaching."

PART I

Developing Instruction
for Students With
Autism Spectrum Disorders

Understanding Students With Autism Spectrum Disorders

Michelle Grenier

• •

One of my primary goals as a teacher is to make sure everyone is included in physical education (PE) and that students with disabilities don't stick out in the classroom. I had the opportunity to test my beliefs two years ago when I had a three-year-old child with ASD enrolled in my program. I was concerned. I had had similar students in the past, but none who were only three years old! How was I going to manage this girl in a large space such as the gym? Fortunately, in our preschool PE program the teachers and aides stay with the class so that our ratio is one adult to every three students.

In preparation for Mary's first day in PE, I placed a hot spot on the floor for her to stand on and attached visuals to a cone that directed her to each station. Although the room divider was lowered to reduce the size of the gymnasium, Mary had little interest in the events that were taking place.

It quickly became apparent that I needed to come up with a game plan that worked. During each class, I got out a balloon and started hitting it in the air as I followed Mary around the gymnasium. She would watch for a few moments and then approach me cautiously, wanting to play. This routine went on for several classes. Every time Mary came to PE, she would run for the other side of the gym, and I would try to entice her back with a balloon or some other object of interest.

I thought about Mary a lot over the next few weeks and decided to mimic everything she did. "If you can't beat them, join them," I resolved. If she lay on the floor, I would lie next to her. If she ran across the gym, I'd run across the gym. The following day, Mary came in and, sure enough, ran to the other side of the curtain. I told her aide to stay and work with the other students in the group as I followed her to the other side. Slowly, my plan began to pay off. Mary started looking my way, "inviting" me to follow here with a ball, balloon, or some other object. A few classes later, our first reciprocal interaction occurred when Mary actually tapped the balloon back to me! I believed that she might now be ready to work with me and her class on the right side of the curtain. I also had her aide work with another group of students.

I knew I needed Mary to recognize me as the person in charge of the class, so I proceeded to enlist her as my helper. Throughout the class, I would stay with Mary and travel with her group to each of the stations. Mary and I would model the stations for the class, and I would deliberately end up at the yoga station because she loves the Do Nothing Doll pose. Whenever she lost interest in what we were doing, I would try to get her back by following her and performing the activity she was supposed to be doing. It took several months to get her into a routine even though the class structure remained the same. The only thing I would change was the station activity. In the beginning, I would keep three activities the same and change only one per week. Gradually, we started changing two activities and eventually worked up to changing three each week. Of the four stations, yoga was the constant because I knew Mary enjoyed this so much.

Throughout this process, I was also aware of the need to establish a relationship with Mary outside of the gym. When I would see Mary in the hall, I would say hi to her. At first she didn't realize who I was because I wasn't where she would typically see me. Over time she started to recognize me in the hallway. She even started saying "Hi, Mrs. Yeaton." I felt that I had finally broken through to her.

How has this all paid off for me? When Mary now comes into the gym with her class, she stands on the line and does a quick warm-up. She still helps me model the stations and enjoys showing her classmates what to do. I am pleased that she is fully integrated into the class. Today, I feel satisfied knowing I've accomplished my learning goals for Mary. It was hard work and required a lot of trial and error, but my reward is that she is now a fully included member of the class.

• •

Mrs. Yeaton, Mary's teacher, would tell you that the most important thing is to get to know your students. Not only does this increase skill and social development, it sends a powerful message to the other students on the importance of treating all students equally.

Like Mrs. Yeaton, teachers need to assume that their students with autism spectrum disorder (ASD) can become contributing class members. Because the skills students demonstrate are continually shifting, teachers should consider not only the abilities of students with ASD, but also the abilities of those around them, who help in shaping their behaviors (Biklen, 2000).

This chapter addresses the primary areas (communication, social relationships, movement, and sensory differences) that affect learning for students with ASD in physical education. The social model is introduced as an alternative to the more traditional medical version of disability to consider ways to overcome barriers and address best practices. In all cases, the focus is always on what the student can do, rather than what they can't, because after all, this is a book for practitioners who are looking for suggestions on how best to instruct students with ASD.

Clinical Definition of Autism Spectrum Disorder

What does it mean when we say a student has ASD? Why use the term *spectrum*? Does a student ever outgrow a diagnosis? Although there are commonalities with the disorder, the spectrum captures, to varying degrees, difficulties in social interaction, communication, and behaviors (Horvat, Kalakian, Croce, & Dahlstrom, 2011).

ASD is a complex disability that once encompassed autistic disorder, Asperger syndrome, pervasive developmental disorder not otherwise specified (PDD-NOS), Rett syndrome, and childhood disintegrative disorder. With the fifth edition of the DSM-5, these subtypes have merged under the umbrella term of ASD. Students with ASD typically struggle with issues in PE such as communication, transitions between activities, and sensory overload. Students diagnosed with Rett syndrome, Williams syndrome, and other disabilities similar to ASD do not always meet the medical criteria for a diagnosis of ASD, but do have learning difficulties that require support.

As a disability, ASD does not discriminate by race or socioeconomic status but tends to occur approximately four times more in males than females. Current estimates from the U.S. Centers for Disease Control (CDC) are that one out of every 88 children will be diagnosed with ASD. A diagnosis of ASD generally indicates difficulties with social interactions, delays in verbal and nonverbal communication, and patterns of atypical behavior such as repetitive or stereotypical movement (*DSM-IV-TR*; American Psychiatric Association, 2000). About 40 percent of students with ASD have average to above average intellectual capabilities, and, although many are nonverbal, communication is possible through assistive technologies and other communication devices.

In addition to the challenges already mentioned, many students with ASD experience difficulties with motor planning, locomotor patterns, and object manipulations that may affect their performance in physical education (Pan, Tsai, & Hsieh, 2011). Given these additional concerns, it is easy to understand why teachers struggle with teaching their students with ASD. It is important, however, to highlight students' strengths because many have unique skills in visual mediums, music, art, history, or math (Kluth, 2010).

Although a label can be helpful for identifying concerns and provide a framework for services, it can also marginalize students (Davis, 1997). A label of ASD should never determine what students learn. Rather, learning should be grounded in students' personal characteristics, abilities, and learning styles. Without actually getting to know the student, what does the label tell you? For some, a label can affect instruction in a negative way (Tripp & Rizzo, 2006). As educators, our goal is to teach all students and to provide experiences that enhance skill and social development. For this reason, this book makes no distinctions among the categories of ASD (e.g., autistic disorder, Rett syndrome, Asperger syndrome) when referring to students on the spectrum.

Practical Manifestations of ASD: Common Characteristics

ASD affects the way students understand the world around them, which makes communication and social interaction a challenge (Kluth, 2010). Many have difficulty negotiating relationships and the nuances of facial gestures and bodily movements. However, it would be a mistake to assume that students with ASD do not want to engage in social relationships simply because they lack the ability to communicate effectively. Stress, a lack of familiarity with the environment, or an inability to share and exchange thoughts can all be contributing factors. They can have difficulty asking questions, which may result in

inappropriate responses that have negative social consequences in the gymnasium. For this reason it is important that teachers work with speech and language therapists to learn how to communicate positively with students with ASD through the use of questions, gestures, and symbols.

Movement patterns may also make it difficult for students with ASD to acquire psychomotor skills. Walking gait may be atypical, or they may engage in repetitive behaviors such as rocking or flapping that make learning a challenge. These behaviors are often accompanied by internal mental thoughts or ruminations that make it difficult to realize individual strengths. With all of this in mind, teachers need to try to avoid making assumptions! Because a student has difficulty in a team sport such as football or basketball does not mean she won't be good in individual sports such as track and field and swimming. Recognizing the implications of stress on movement behaviors is helpful in designing a space that will alleviate some of these external stressors.

Attention is another area that challenges teachers in their efforts to engage students with ASD. Common behaviors include difficulties transitioning to new activities, lack of attention to specific tasks that do not interest the student, and overattention to preferred activities. Helping students attend to specific tasks in PE can be accomplished through a variety of means. Teachers can print figures and symbols on a card, use iPad applications, or simply manipulate the student through the skill so he becomes familiar with the movement (see figure 1.1).

FIGURE 1.1 Students have a card that shows them how to do the task, and a leader models for the other students.

Sensory differences, or an oversensitivity to smell, touch, sound, or movement, may trigger unwanted behaviors such as rocking, spinning, and hand flapping. In addition to vision and hearing modalities, tactile, vestibular, and proprioceptive modalities make up the primary sensory areas essential for experiencing and responding within a given context (Horvat, Kalakian, Croce, & Dahlstrom, 2011). For example, many students with ASD do not like bright, fluorescent gymnasium lights. Hats, hoods, and even visors can minimize these environmental effects. External sounds such as a fire alarm or other emergency drills can cause a meltdown. Teachers should try to prepare ahead and use consistent classroom routines to lessen students' anxiety that can affect their behavior. One way to do this is to minimize light or sound intensity. Students can be directed to areas where they can calm down and be given a menu of visually appropriate behaviors that will help ease their stress.

Communication issues vary depending on the intellectual, social, and emotional capacities of the student. Primary areas encompass expressive, receptive, and ritualized language. What this means is that students may have trouble sharing their thoughts or have difficulty understanding what is being asked of them (Merges, 2011). Many have difficulty with spoken language and with understanding sentence meaning, intonation, and rhythm. Some have a speech form called echolalia, which is the repetition or echoing of verbal utterances made by another person, whereas others repeat speech patterns with no particular meaning. Many higher-functioning students with ASD communicate quite well, whereas others rarely speak or speak in a static, dry tone. Development of speaking and writing skills can be uneven. Some read but do not demonstrate an understanding or comprehension of terminology. This inability to communicate effectively can be a significant barrier to learning in the gymnasium.

Social Model of Disability

This book adopts the social model of disability as a way of understanding teaching practices and how practitioners can respond to the challenges of working with students who have disabilities. Oftentimes, the dominant model used in physical education for such students is grounded in the idea that they are in many ways inferior to their peers (Grenier, 2007). In some cases the environ-ment itself prohibits student performance, hence disabling them. Our belief is that teacher attitudes are shaped by cultural conditions that position students with disabilities in less-than-optimal positions (Block & Obrusnikova, 2007). The social model removes the medical analysis of disability by allowing students to be valued in relationship to their functional ability rather than their medical profile.

Supporting students with ASD means taking a close look at the environment, applying teaching skills that best meet the needs of the students, and using an environmental design approach that reconfigures supports (Block, 2007). Analyzing teaching practices from this perspective shifts the responsibility for participation from the person to the person within the context, which is particularly important in physical education. A contextually based model for learning in the physical education setting, which is referenced in this book, addresses ways to differentiate teaching, the use of appropriate equipment, and an ecological inventory of features within the environment that can support learning. One of the best pieces of advice for working with students with ASD can be illustrated in the sidebar.

Inclusion for Students With ASD

Inclusion of students with disabilities in physical education emerged from legislation developed in response to the discriminatory practices of educational exclusion. The Education for All Handicapped Children Act (EHA) was passed in 1975 and reauthorized as the Individuals with Disabilities Education Act (IDEA) in 1990, 1997, and 2004. The law outlined the need for individualized plans of instruction, inclusion in the general education classroom to the greatest extent appropriate, and parental input in making decisions.

In addition to providing guidelines for identifying and educating students with disabilities in the general classroom, the law also articulated school systems' responsibility for physically educating the child with disabilities. By definition, students with disabilities, as specifically named in the Education for All Handicapped Children Act, are required to have physical education, as noted in the following passage that defines the term *special education*:

What You Can Learn From Students

A picture is worth a thousand words, and I can vouch for that! It was one of the first days of school, and I was going over fire drill procedures, bathroom procedures, and gymnasium rules with a class of third graders. We were also creating a portfolio cover for collecting student papers for the year. The instructions for the task were to draw a picture on the cover that illustrated a favorite sport or activity. As I walked around the gym to see what students were drawing, I noticed that a couple of the boys were laughing at one boy's picture, glancing around to check on my whereabouts. I went over and looked at what John, who had ASD, had drawn. To my surprise, it was a man-eating cat with large claws, bloodshot eyes, a spiked tail, and a radar gun on its back. In its mouth was a stick figure, and I knew instantly whom that represented. It was me! The figure had a basketball in its hand and a word bubble that said "Blah, blah, blah." I was so mad that I called the school guidance counselor to process the picture with John.

Later that evening, after I had had a chance to calm down, I realized that John was trying to tell me something—that I talked too much. When I actually reflected on what went on in class, I had probably been "blah, blah, blahing" for about half an hour. That was a *long* time, especially in a class in which students are expected to move. The something that needed to change was not John and his drawings; it was me talking too much!

You never know when the tables will turn and you will become the learner, and your student, the teacher. Nine years later I still have his portfolio cover in my office to remind me to keep things simple.

The cover of the student's portfolio.

The term *special education* means specially designed instruction, at no cost to the parents, to meet the unique needs of a child with a disability including classroom instruction, *instruction in physical education* [emphasis added], home instruction, and instruction in hospitals and institutions. (Federal Register, August 23, 1977, p. 42480)

Lawmakers further articulated the importance of physical education, as follows:

The Committee is concerned that although these services are available to and required of all children in our school systems, they are often viewed as a luxury for handicapped children. (Federal Register, August 23, 1977, p. 42489)

Students with ASD are one of the most segregated groups; 44 percent of students with ASD spend 60 percent of their day outside the general education setting (U.S. Department of Education, 2009). Student placement is a condition of the least restrictive environment (LRE) clause, which specifies that, whenever possible, students with disabilities should be educated in the same environments as their peers. Placement options can vary depending on the school, the teachers, and the resources. Primary concerns include the child's educational programming and whether it best meets the child's educational needs. It is important to remember that students with disabilities should only be removed from class "when the nature or severity of the disability is such that education in regular classes with the use of supplementary aids

and services cannot be achieved satisfactorily" (IDEA, PL 101-476, ξ 612[a][5]). For some students this means having an adapted physical education program, whereas others may be included in the general physical education program.

Placement decisions should be made by professionals familiar with a variety of assessments. The most recent recommendation is that students must score 1.5 standard deviations below the norm to qualify for services (American Association for Physical Activity and Recreation, 2010). Even teachers who are not familiar with these testing guidelines should remember that service and supports are necessary for any successful program. Their experience working with a specific child with ASD and an understanding of interventions that have been effective in the past will help teachers identify placement criteria and optimal instructional strategies.

Schools have a responsibility to try to provide access to the general education curriculum for all students. However, they differ in their approaches to inclusion. The checklist in figure 1.2 can be used to analyze whether placement conditions support inclusive practices.

Checklist for Inclusion of Students in Physical Education

☐ Is there a school philosophy that supports students with disabilities?

☐ Does the school leadership provide training and support for the staff to teach in ways that maximize learning opportunities for all students?

☐ Are students being educated with peers?

☐ If not, what criteria were used to make that determination?

☐ Is there open communication between the PE/APE teacher and other educators such as paraprofessionals, occupational therapists, case managers, and speech therapists?

☐ Do special and general educators collaborate to ensure that students have access to supports and services?

☐ Do students with ASD have access to the same curriculum as students without disabilities?

☐ Do students with ASD participate in extracurricular activities?

☐ Does the physical education program provide an accessible curriculum for students with a range of abilities?

☐ Do the lessons follow a progression of differentiated instruction?

☐ Are community and recreational sports available to students with ASD to provide opportunities for physical and social engagement?

FIGURE 1.2   Checklist to determine the degree of inclusion and how to be more inclusive.

How Does This All Play Out?

Determining where and how to educate a student with ASD has much to do with the teacher's experience and knowledge of disability (Block, 2007; Sherrill, 2004). Some states, such as California, require that an endorsed adapted physical education teacher provide instruction to students requiring an adaptive setting. Many others states simply rely on the general physical education teacher to provide direct instruction to such students. At the local level, resources and the teacher's ability to accommodate students with ASD often determine the success of the student in the gymnasium.

A definition of inclusion should include meaningful participation, equal treatment of all students, access to the physical education curriculum, and the opportunity to work with peers. When considering the most appropriate environment for students, teachers should ensure that these criteria are met. Because so many teachers lack fundamental knowledge of disability teaching practices, professional development in the schools should be used to prepare all staff members, not just those who show an interest in teaching students with disabilities in either general or adapted settings. Teachers can request that the school provide access to personnel familiar with students with ASD to learn how best to educate them in physical education. Collaborating with related service providers can garner much information on effective strategies for communicating and minimizing stress in the classroom.

Conclusion

The last decade has seen an increased awareness of ASD, what it means to have ASD, and teaching practices that best address the needs of students with ASD. Because this book is written as a primer, it is not a "cookbook" for success. The supports needed to ensure success depend on the student and his or her level of experience, as well as the abilities of the teacher. As Rick Rogers, a veteran high school teacher, points out:

> A program is only as good and exciting as the person who teaches it. The educator who is passionate about what he or she is doing has the ability to elicit more positive outcomes than the teacher who is moderately invested. Passionate educators create lasting gains in subject matter, but more important, they create an environment that is accepting and values individual differences. The energy that flows from a passionate educator is felt by all class members and acts a catalyst to exceed expectations. (Personal communication)

Given the growing incidence of children diagnosed with ASD, the chances are that many PE teachers will have students with ASD in their gymnasiums. To meet their needs, teachers need to be aware of the characteristics of ASD. However, they should not let those characteristics define the student. They should remember to look at each student as an individual and be prepared to bring the best practices to their classroom to benefit all students. The same teaching strategies that enhance participation for the student with ASD, such as the use of visuals in the classroom and consistency with routines, will also support students not identified on the spectrum. Good teaching for one student is good teaching for every student.

Autism Spectrum Disorders From the Family Perspective

Teri Todd and Ann Griffin

• •

Shopping trips to the local big-box store have become a family favorite. Wide aisles, high ceilings, and not too much noise create an environment that David can tolerate. And bonus— pizza at the end of the trip! David is talkative and having fun helping choose items and placing them in the cart. He is patient at the checkout line, eyeing the pizza counter just on the other side. I give him the pizza money and we head toward the counter. "Be careful; it is right out of the oven," the person serving the pizza tells David. As we walk toward the table, David lets his plate slant down on one side. As the cheese begins to slip off, all hell breaks loose! Cheese is supposed to be on top of the pizza!

We make it to the table and put the plate down, and I say aloud to both of us, "Breathe. We can fix this." But all David can see is the cheese askew on the pizza. He bangs his head with his fist, screams loudly, and drops to the floor. The man at the next table asks how old he is. I answer as I try to contain my inconsolable child, "He is eight." "More like two if you ask me," the man replies. I want to cry. "He has autism," I say. The man looks at me blankly, picks up his meal, and leaves the store. The people nearby continue to stare. I kneel down beside David. "Breathe, Honey, we can fix this." No luck. I stand up and ask my husband to toss the food in the garbage. Together, we struggle to get our son to stand and leave.

• •

Families typically enjoy participating in school fairs, sporting events, and outdoor activities, just as David's family enjoys shopping. But these trips can be real challenges for families with a child with autism spectrum disorder (ASD) because of a variety of sensory and behavioral difficulties. This chapter outlines some of the challenges that parents of children with ASD encounter and ways general and adapted physical education teachers can help both parents and children adopt an active lifestyle. Understanding the concerns, stress level, and fears of parents of children with ASD can help teachers understand why parents might be defensive during IEP meetings, for example.

Stress and the Parent

Parents encounter many stressful situations while raising their children. Whether a child is having a meltdown at the grocery store, refusing to perform a chore, or feeling upset because of not making a team, parents must deal with the repercussions. The unique blend of challenges faced by children with ASD make social outings difficult and can lead to feelings of social isolation for parents. They may stay away from public settings for fear that their child will display challenging or odd behaviors and face discrimination or rejection. It is not surprising that parents of children with ASD experience high levels of stress and are at increased risk for poor mental health, "not only from the demands of caring for a child with ASD but also other stressors which are exacerbated by their child's disability" (Meadan, Halle, & Ebata, 2010, p. 21).

Many parents cope with such stress by avoiding the public arena. Sometimes this can be extreme, as in the case of a family that built a high wall around the house so their child could not run away and neighbors would not witness meltdowns. Even though limiting public outings may alleviate immediate stress, it is not an optimal solution. Isolation decreases the potential for social support, and social support is one of the strongest mediators for stress reduction. It is not surprising, too, that parental stress, in particular maternal stress, is related to the severity of the child's behavioral problems. The more behavioral problems a child displays, the greater the impact on the parent.

Research has demonstrated that parents of children with ASD experience higher levels of stress and lower levels of well-being than parents of children without ASD or any other type of disability (Baker-Ericzen, Brookman-Frazee, & Stahmer, 2005). Particularly challenging for parents are the characteristics of their children's disorder, such as frustration with communication, overstimulation, and challenging behavior (Baker, Blacher, Crnic, & Edelbrock, 2002).

It is easy to see why parents of a child with ASD may appear at their wits' end on many occasions. The constant demand of parenting a child with ASD leaves little time for relaxation, exercise, or hobbies, all of which contribute to a positive quality of life. In addition, parents of children with ASD experience stressful events daily. Smith and colleagues (2010) found that the number of daily stressors was related to higher negative and lower positive affect; when a child is having a challenging day, the parent is negatively affected.

People cope with stress in a variety of ways, some more effectively than others. The match between a specific stressor and the coping response determines coping effectiveness. Certain coping responses have been associated with positive outcomes for parents of children with ASD. However, other coping strategies frequently used by parents lead to negative outcomes. Two researchers recently studied the effect of 12 coping strategies by parents of children with ASD (Pottie & Ingram, 2008). They found that the personality of the parent and the context of the event influenced the effectiveness of the strategy. However,

with those results notwithstanding, certain strategies proved more effective than other in reducing parent stress and improving well-being. Table 2.1 shows a list of the coping strategies and outcomes.

Helping Parents Cope

Teachers can help parents and families by learning to recognize the coping strategy parents have chosen. Frequently, parents choose strategies that are effective and lead to positive outcomes for everyone. However, some parents engage in less effective coping strategies that only increase their stress and make it more difficult to resolve the situation.

Recognizing an ineffective strategy allows the educator to remain objective and, if possible, model an effective one. Consider a teacher who is frustrated because a mother is not following through on a recommendation. When asked about this, the mother immediately begins blaming someone or something else. The teacher can be objective and recognize that the mother is in a stressful situation and engaging in a coping strategy that decreases her well-being. From this place, the teacher can model a positive coping strategy such as a problem-focused approach or one that involves social supports.

Successful PE inclusion programs require ongoing communication between parents and teachers. Parents seek out educators who want family involvement and are willing to communicate with them on a regular basis. Communication refers to giving information to parents and listening to what they have to say. Do you model good communication? (See sidebar titled Are You a Family-Friendly Educator?) The next section outlines some important ways teachers can help parents in their efforts to promote physical activity.

Opening the Lines of Communication for Parents

Effective, ongoing communication between parents and teachers is essential for effective program development, sound instructional planning, and student success. Teachers can open the lines of communication with the family by offering information about the program and the benefits of physical education. They can inform parents about the importance of physical activity in their children's lives for increasing overall health and decreasing negative behaviors. A review of

TABLE 2.1   Parental Coping Strategies and Outcomes

Strategies	Improves well-being and decreases stress	Decreases well-being
Problem focused: taking action to deal with a difficult or stressful situation in a concrete or organized manner	✔	
Social support: reaching out to others for emotional and/or practical/concrete assistance	✔	
Escape or avoidance: removing or disengaging oneself from the stressful situation, or refusing to accept the reality of the situation		✔
Distraction: dealing with a stressful situation by engaging in an alternative pleasurable activity or self-care	✔	
Blaming: actions that involve frustration, anger, blaming, or passive aggression		✔
Positive reframing: changing one's view of a stressful situation in order to see it in a positive/more tolerable light	✔	
Worrying: constant or frequent thinking about the negative or difficult aspects of a stressful situation		✔
Emotional regulation: controlling or expressing emotional distress in a way that is constructive or appropriate for the situation	✔	
Withdrawal: staying away from certain people or preventing others from knowing about the stressful situation or its emotional effects		✔
Compromise: working out a compromise between the priorities/needs of the individual and the limits of the stressful situation	✔	
Helplessness: giving up or surrendering control because the stressor was/is overwhelming		✔

Pottie and Ingram 2008.

Modeling a Positive Coping Strategy

The parents of Carly, who is one of your fifth-grade students, are worried because they fear she will be ridiculed in her general physical education class. Her mother explains that she is afraid Carly will display behaviors that will cause other children to laugh at or be annoyed with her. This could result in ostracism or ridicule. As her physical education (PE) teacher, you see the positive opportunities of inclusion and feel confident that you can create a supportive environment by providing disability awareness discussions with the other students before Carly's arrival to the class. This will minimize the risk of a negative outcome and provide opportunities for students to volunteer as peer tutors. You explain to Carly's mother that you will take concrete action to support Carly in physical education and invite the mother to join you during a disability awareness discussion. As Carly's educator, you have demonstrated a problem-focused approach and provided an opportunity for her mother to adopt this positive coping strategy.

Are You a Family-Friendly Educator?

Mark the statements that apply to you, to discover how family-friendly you are as an educator.

____ I can identify various coping strategies.
____ I model positive coping techniques.
____ I communicate regularly with the family.
____ I find out what activities interest the whole family.
____ I consult the family in program development.
____ I provide the family with relevant reports prior to an IEP meeting.
____ I involve the family in setting IEP goals.
____ I invite the family to school and community events and outings.
____ I share the student's success with the family.

research related to the benefits of exercise for people with ASD conducted by Dawson and Rosonoff at Autism Speaks revealed the following:

> Besides improving fitness, motor function, and behavior in individuals with autism, among the most important advantages of physical activity are the social implications of participating in sports and exercise. Physical activity can promote self-esteem, increase general levels of happiness, and can lead to positive social outcomes, all highly beneficial outcomes for individuals with autism. (Dawson & Rosonoff)

Teachers can help parents cope with their children's behaviors by encouraging the creation of physical education and adapted physical education classes uniquely suited to their concerns.

Listening to Parents

Parents can offer valuable insights into their children because they know their interests, fears, dislikes, triggers, and needs, and therefore, the challenges teachers can face (Kozub, 2008). The following passage illustrates some of the difficulties parents face:

> It takes great patience and perseverance and imagination to teach a child like Bridgette. My daughter is severely autistic, quite obese, headstrong, and difficult to reach. . . . Bridgette is capable of very aggressive behavior, pushing, biting, and pinching. (Personal communication from a parent)

Physical educators should seek information from parents about their children's preferences for toys, equipment, items, or subjects. What particular things bother the child, or tend to trigger meltdowns or behavioral blowups? It is wise, also, to learn from parents what *not* to do. One student named Dalton hated to be told to get a partner, a fairly common direction in physical education. It caused him to get really mad and run out of the gym. Dalton's parents were called about the situation. They explained how he does not like to *get a partner*. Once Dalton's teacher understood that this was associated with bad experiences at his last school, the teacher was able to avoid this situation by choosing a PE partner for Dalton before class.

Offering Feedback

General or adapted physical education teachers can give parents updates about their children in the form of success stories such as a positive notes, digital photos, or YouTube video links posted from an iPad. This communication should always be positive. Parents can be involved in the program by attending special culminating events that help the student generalize to a community setting, such as at a bowling alley or roller skating rink. This can be a wonderful opportunity for parents to enjoy time with their children. Here is a note from a parent who had received a video of her daughter performing a routine in PE classes. The passage illustrates what can occur when teachers and parents keep an open dialogue.

> I received a videotape in the mail of Brianna's physical education class. While

watching that tape, I began to cry. . . . I saw the teacher teaching Brianna to enjoy physical exercise, something I didn't really know if we could get her to really try again.

Ongoing Communication and the IEP Process

Physical education is part of the student's individual education plan (IEP), which is designed to ensure that student gets the supports and services they need to make progress in physical education class. IEP teams are composed of school administrators, teachers, parents, and special education support staff who may be working with the student or family. Members meet on an annual basis to review goals, student progress, and services. They collaborate and problem solve to customize the IEP. Teachers can be very helpful in setting the tone of IEP meetings by providing parents with relevant reports on the student's motor skills, fitness testing, or leisure preferences prior to the meeting. Parents' information can inform instructional planning because, in many cases, they are the experts on their children (Kozub, 2008). Parents, like the professionals on the team, should receive reports and information prior to the meeting.

IEP goals should be written to target skills that will enable the family to engage in leisure activities together (see figure 2.1 for examples).

Goals and Short-Term Objectives for the IEP

Sample annual goals describing the scope and focus of the physical education program

- Laurie will increase strength, flexibility, eye–hand coordination, motor skills, and social interaction through participation in physical education.
- Susan will increase leisure skills through participation in a variety of recreational activities on and off campus (disc golf, roller skating, ice skating, tennis, and fitness walking).
- Brian will generalize leisure skills acquired to community recreation facilities (YMCA fitness center, bowling alley, disc golf courses at city parks, roller rink, ice arena).

Sample short-term objectives describing specific instructional targets

They are written in behavioral terms, also known as SMART goals. (SMART stands for specific, measurable, achievable, realistic, and time frame.)

- Upon verbal request, Gabe will demonstrate three of the following locomotor patterns without physical assistance and for a distance of 10 feet (3 m): hop, jump, leap, skip, gallop.
- Given a tag stick, Gabe will participate in tag game for five minutes tagging his peers with a light touch on the shoulder, back, or arm.
- Bryanna will play catch with a partner standing 15 feet (4.6 m) away for five minutes of continuous activity using a variety of items.
- Graham will ride a bicycle in control: starting, stopping, and turning, for 20 or more minutes.
- Ryan will independently interact with three classmates, two out of three days.
- Richard will identify five exercise machines he enjoys at the YMCA and learn how to use them correctly with appropriate weight, repetitions, and time.
- At the local bowling alley, Joe will score an average of 130 in three consecutive games.
- Jasmine will participate in a weekly bowling program at Rose Bowling Lanes. She will pay for the outing, ask for bowling shoes, find the correct lane, complete one game, return bowling shoes, and leave the bowling alley quietly.

FIGURE 2.1 The IEP should include goals and objectives related to involving the family outside of school to enhance social connections and skill practice.

Parents who enjoy softball are more likely to work on batting practice with their child. Likewise, families who enjoy cycling can spend time teaching their child to ride a bicycle knowing that this can be a future family event. When families are part of the decision process, they are more likely to involve their children in after-school activities, which can help build social connections.

During the middle and high school years, IEP teams are increasingly focused on transition goals, preparing the student for life after high school. During this time students and their families directly benefit from collaborative program planning. Educators should be aware of recreation services in the community and build transition goals that incorporate these resources. To encourage recreation within the community, teachers can tailor instructional programs to include the skills required to participate with family and friends in activities outside of class.

Conclusion

Families of children with ASD want to have fun together, but this can be difficult because of the unique challenges faced by their children. Physical educators can be instrumental in making this happen. One parent stated: "Our physical education teacher has helped us have fun as a family, 'tricking' us into challenging our previous physical and mental limitations" (personal communication). Understanding the unique stresses involved in raising a child with ASD can help teachers communicate effectively with the family. They can be objective when parents are struggling to cope and even act as role models. By teaching activities that can become proactive coping strategies to decrease stress for the family, teachers contribute to student success. Family-friendly educators partner with families, identify activities everyone enjoys, and teach their students the skills required to engage in lifelong pursuits.

Accessing the Curriculum Through the Inclusion Spectrum

Michelle Grenier

· ·

After a one-year absence due to illness, Brian, a nonverbal 10-year-old student with autism spectrum disorder (ASD), was to return to his physical education class. In preparation for his arrival, his physical education teacher, Mrs. Manning, had prearranged teams for the cooperative learning (CL) lessons she was going to implement. In addition to her careful selection of the groups, she also took the time to create a visual planner and lesson plan. The visual planner included the CL jobs (coach, equipment manager, encourager, task reader, and recorder) with a short description and a photo of Brian performing each one. The lesson plan included images of Brian's classmates working through the activities. Next, team folders were assembled that contained the task sheets, contracts, and job responsibilities. Mrs. Manning then positioned the color-coded folders and the equipment needed for the class in a designated area of the gymnasium.

After entering the gym, Brian quickly took his place on the end line with his classmates as Mrs. Manning announced the new cooperative learning groups. Once that was completed, Brian and the other three students in his group proceeded to pick up their team folder and found their places in the back corner of the gymnasium. After the four students reviewed the task sheets, they signed the contract indicating a commitment to meet the learning goals.

As the equipment manager, Brian was responsible for marking the playing area with cones. He had the support of one of his group members, who walked him through the routine, helping him position the cones in each of the four corners. From there, Brian's group completed the warm-up portion of the lesson under the coach's direction. Having successfully completed the warm-ups, Brian and his group spent the remainder of the class working through the task sheet.

Each day Brian's routine in physical education (PE) class followed a similar pattern. In addition, he would preview the lesson plan task sheet with his paraprofessional prior to the start of class. This familiarized him with the routine and helped him understand his daily role (Grenier & Yeaton, 2011).

On those PE days when Brian lost focus and became agitated, Mrs. Manning quickly intervened, allowing him to shoot baskets. This preferred activity was used to motivate Brian. "Complete the task and you can shoot 10 baskets" was a common phrase Mrs. Manning used. After a minute of this, his peers would encourage him to reenter the group. "We need you, Brian, to do the next activity" was all they needed to say. Their support and positive interactions were motivating factors for his participation in PE.

· ·

This chapter describes the inclusion spectrum and how teachers can use it to organize instruction (Stevenson, 2009). Teachers can choose among open, modified, parallel, separate, and disability sport activities, based on any number of factors including the student, the class, and the content they are teaching. Mrs. Manning's cooperative learning lesson would be considered a parallel activity on the inclusion spectrum. In her lesson she grouped students according to their abilities and learning characteristics, which enabled them to progress at their own pace (Johnson & Johnson, 1991). Visual support, such as previewing the lesson by looking at pictures of himself performing the tasks, helped ease Brian's transition into the lesson. Group members took responsibility for their behaviors by signing a contract. A job sheet listing student roles scripted their behaviors. Wall posters described the various jobs (see figure 3.1) to remind students of their

tasks, and a notebook containing visuals of all of the jobs was available as a reference. Independent group work allowed Mrs. Manning to monitor the class and help anyone who needed it. Most important was the support Brian received from his peers as they helped him navigate the tasks by prompting and guiding his actions, making it possible for him to adjust to the daily changes. The next section addresses the significance of the inclusion spectrum within PE and provides examples of ways it can be applied to include students with ASD.

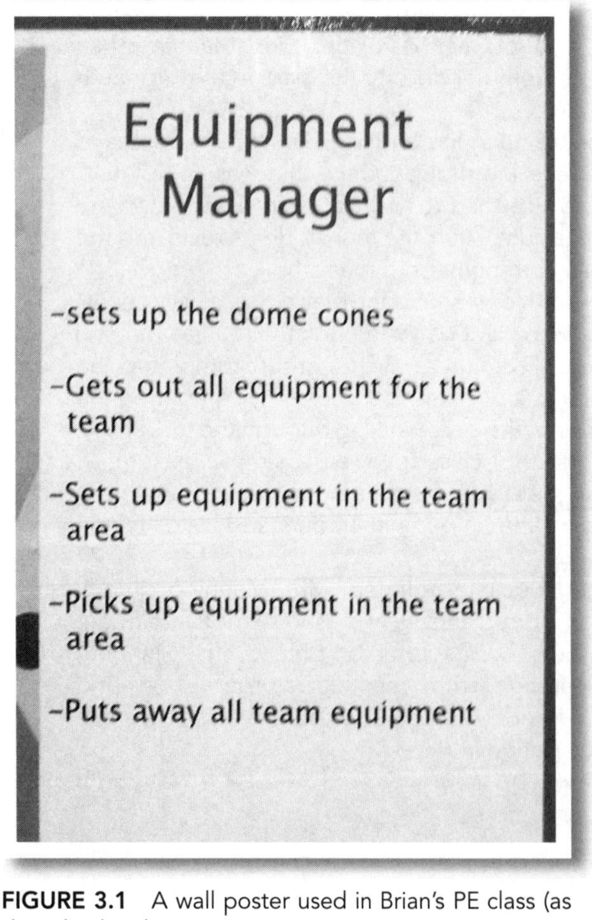

The Inclusion Spectrum

One of the primary challenges facing physical education teachers is addressing the needs of a wide variety of students. Because students with ASD have issues that may affect their ability to be successful in physical education, the inclusion spectrum can be applied as a teaching tool to structure content in way that supports a variety of learning abilities (Stevenson, 2009).

The inclusion spectrum uses an inclusive design that enables teachers to understand, within given contexts, how to address the learning needs of each of their students. One advantage of the spectrum is that it creates opportunities for students to work with their peers (Broderick, Mehta-Parekh, & Reid, 2005). Depending on the learning objectives of the lesson, the teacher may instruct all students in the same manner using a similar organizational setup, particularly if the activity allows for a wide variation of movement options such as a dance unit or a unit addressing basic throwing and catching skills. In other cases, the teacher can organize students by ability, interest, or personality to accomplish learning goals.

In the opening scenario, Mrs. Manning used cooperative learning to have students in Brian's class work together at their own pace according to their own needs. At other times, she might choose a modified game with specialized equipment or rule changes that would enable Brian to participate with his class. This would depend on what she wanted to accomplish in the class.

Joseph Winnick (2011) originally developed the inclusion spectrum in 1987 as a schematic to illustrate placement options within the condition of the least restrictive environment (see figure 3.2). A spectrum of placement possibilities makes it easy for teachers to visualize their choices.

FIGURE 3.1 A wall poster used in Brian's PE class (as described in the opening scenario).

Levels 1 and 2 include participation in regular sport settings such as physical education and intramural and extramural activities. At level 3, students engage in sports that include people with and without disabilities, such as a wheelchair athlete competing in a running event for people without disabilities. At level 4, athletes with and without disabilities compete in the same sport (e.g., wheelchair basketball). At level 5, those with disabilities compete in sports specifically designed for them. Each Saturday morning, for example, the University of New Hampshire offers power soccer for anyone using a power chair.

In 1996, Ken Black took Winnick's continuum for sport participation and modified it to give teachers more flexibility in how they group students (see figure 3.3). The main alteration was to give each component equal importance. In essence, it transformed a hierarchical placement structure into an instructional tool for grouping

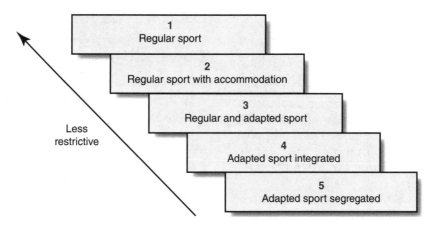

FIGURE 3.2 An integration continuum for sport participation.

Reprinted, by permission, from J.P. Winnick, 1987, "An integration continuum for sport participation," *Physical Activity Quarterly* 4(3): 157-161.

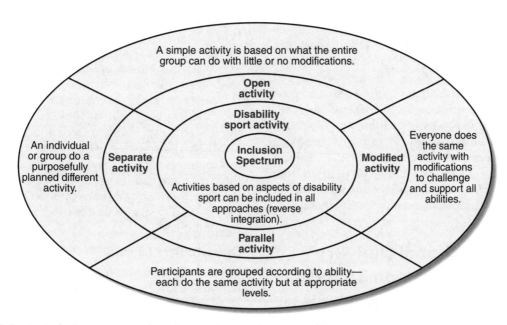

FIGURE 3.3 An inclusion spectrum that gives each component equal importance.

Reprinted, by permission, from K. Black and D. Williamson, 2011, Designing inclusive physical activities and games. In *Design for sport*, edited by A.C. Roibas, E. Stamatakis, and K. Black (Burlington, VT: Ashgate Publishing Company).

students and customizing instruction (Black & Williamson, 2011).

Planning Process for Using the Inclusion Spectrum

Before using the inclusion spectrum, teachers must consider the content they are teaching and how the selected games or activities can be structured so that all students can participate at their own ability levels. Lifetime leisure skills and community-based activities such as bowling, weight training, golf, snowshoeing, swimming, tennis, and biking can be especially helpful for students with ASD. These students often have greater success in individual sports than they do in team sports because the movement patterns are less complex and involve fewer transitions. Many physical education programs offer climbing walls, cardio rooms, wrestling rooms, and pools that can give students opportunities to participate in recreational activities that can extend beyond their schooling years.

Students with ASD should not be an afterthought in the planning process. Their participation levels should be equal to those of their classmates. Although their learning goals may be different from those of their classmates depending on their individual education plans (IEPs), access to the curriculum is a requirement of the law. This does not mean that they will necessarily be performing the same activities as their peers, but they should be participating in meaningful and age-appropriate activities. The same issues that cause problems with other children will also pose a challenge for students with ASD such as inadequate equipment, lack of routine, and too much time spent waiting for class to start (Graham, Holt/Hale, & Parker, 2009). Physical education should be a collaborative process that involves input from key players such as the special education teacher and speech, occupational, and physical therapists.

Instructional Delivery Using the Inclusion Spectrum

Five activity categories comprise the inclusion spectrum. *Open* activities are those that require little or no modifications to include all students.

Modified activities are those that include everyone, with modifications or supports for certain students. *Parallel* activities involve grouping students according to ability; everyone performs the same skill or activity but at various levels. *Separate* activities are purposely planned for individuals or groups that require skill development lessons that differs from those of the students in the general curriculum. *Disability sports,* or reverse integration, activities are designed for people with disabilities. Within any given class structure, teachers may use more than one category of the inclusion spectrum depending on the student, the class, and the content.

Open Activities

Open activities are the most fluid of all the activities in the inclusion spectrum. In the open format, no modifications are necessary because the attributes generally lend themselves to the inclusion of all students. Consider, for example, a game of partner tag, which involves the skills of chasing and fleeing. Students can opt to move in their own way at their own speed particularly when the teacher uses commands such as "Move" rather than "Run."

Open Activity Example 1: Partner Tag

Everyone finds a partner. On the signal, partners move around the gymnasium and avoid getting tagged as they try to tag another pair of partners. When this happens, each pair switches roles. Chasers become fleers and fleers become chasers. The open end of the inclusion spectrum allows students the flexibility to move in their own ways. It involves a significant amount of teaching by invitation, which enables them to move according to their own abilities (Mosston & Ashworth, 2002). Students with ASD can choose their means and methods of partnering with other students, or their partners can be preselected by the teacher. Because there are minimal task limitations, students' varying speeds and ways of moving can be accommodated.

Open Activity Example 2: Dribbling Skills

On the teacher's command, "Everyone get a ball and start moving around," everyone in the class selects a ball and starts traveling around the gymnasium. Students can elect the type of ball and the way they propel it. Students with

Partner tag is a type of open activity because it allows students the flexibility to move in their own ways.

learning materials that help students make sense of ideas regardless of their differences in ability. It is important to note that some of the modifications may be specific to the student with ASD, whereas others may involve the entire class such as a rule change or an equipment choice for everyone.

When modifying activities, physical educators need to consider the physical capacities of their students and the primary social challenges these capacities entail. Although some may be able to move quickly through a series of progressions, others, perhaps those with sensory overload or motor challenges, may not be able to accomplish the task at the same speed as their classmates. Typically teachers use one of two approaches to skill analysis. They may adopt a developmental, or bottom-up, approach whereby the student progresses from easier to more difficult skills (Block, 2007; Sherrill, 2004). For example, if a student is not able to hit a target using a racket, he could use his hand to strike. An alternative to this is the ecological approach, in which the task is analyzed according to its outcomes. In this method, the teacher focuses on the goal (getting the ball to the target) rather than the process of getting it there (using proper throwing technique). In this case, the student simply needs to find a way to get the ball to hit the target, either by throwing or striking. Modifications at the instructional level may include the use of visual supports or social stories to help students with ASD better comprehend the task.

Modified Activity Example 1: Jump Rope

While some students are participating in a jump rope activity using the full circular swing, others may elect to jump over ropes placed on the floor or ropes that swing only halfway. Some may need hand-to-hand support while jumping, and others may be able to execute the skill without any physical support. This is an example of a skill modification that uses the developmental approach.

Modified Activity Example 2: Social Stories

One primary modification for students with ASD is the use of social stories and visual scripts. Social stories may be used to head off a potential outburst, and scripts can be used to ease the transition into physical education. An example of this is provided in the opening scenario. This is an example of an instructional approach to support student learning.

limited skill can simply walk with the ball. More advanced students can dribble the ball. Typically during open activities, movement concepts—such as moving quickly or slowly, or at high or low levels—(Graham et al., 2009) can be applied to give versatility to the skill without compromising the integrity of the activity.

Modified Activities

Modifying the skill, activity, or game allows students with ASD to display their skills through the use of differentiation and equipment modification (Ellis, Lieberman, & LeRoux, 2009). Differentiation involves the use of teaching strategies and

Parallel Activities

In parallel activities of the inclusion spectrum, all students are generally practicing the same skill or activity, but are grouped according to ability level. In many cases, students can begin the class with either an open or modified activity; then, as the class moves toward more game play, the teacher can use the parallel method to organize teams. Consider how athletes are grouped according to their skill levels in pool lanes. Slower swimmers are assigned specific lanes, and others are grouped together according to their speed. This makes it easy for more people to swim in a lane and for coaches to target swimmers' developmental levels.

Parallel Activity Example 1: Volleyball

Students can elect to participate in a variety of game options for volleyball. Some may choose the traditional six versus six game with a standard ball. A second group may elect to use a volleyball trainer and a variety of options for serving. Another group may decide to play a game of sitting volleyball. All three groups are participating in the game of volleyball, each according to the ability level of its member.

Parallel Activity Example 2: Goalball

In this example, the teacher creates three groupings for the game of goalball. The first group sits in a circle on the floor and uses a large ball with bells. A second group rolls a standard goalball around their legs as they stand in a circle. None of the participants are wearing eyeshades. The third group performs the same skills as those in the first two groups, but they are wearing eyeshades. Note that this is both a parallel activity and a disability sport.

Separate Activities

There are many ways to envision separate activities. Students in adapted physical education programs outside the general physical education setting can be supported with previewing and preteaching activities. The goals for students in separate, specialized schools may be very different from those of students in traditional physical education programs. Typically, the focus of separate activities is lifetime activities.

Separate Activity Example 1: Skiing

Students with severe ASD who are enrolled in schools specifically designed for their needs may participate in activities such as adapted ski programs. In the photo, the student is using a sit ski while his instructors control his speed using tethers. This physical activity is specifically designed to introduce this student to a sport he can enjoy for a lifetime.

An adapted ski program provides a skill that can result in enjoyment for a lifetime.

Separate Activity Example 2: Adapted Physical Education

A student with ASD who is overly sensitive to the noise in a gymnasium may totally withdraw from any level of participation. In this case, her IEP team may decide that her unique needs warrant a specially designed physical education program that focuses on sensory integration and activities such as rocking in a cylinder or using various types of balls to enhance gripping and manipulation skills.

Disability Sport Activities

Given the popularity of the Paralympic movement and the increase in the numbers of disability sport teams at the recreational and intercollegiate levels, disability sports are an attractive addition to any physical education program (Davis, 2011). Some,

Wheelchair basketball can level the playing field because students without disabilities often need to learn new skills.

such as goalball and sledge hockey, are unique to a disability, whereas others, such as wheelchair basketball and sitting volleyball, are modifications of their traditional counterparts. One advantage of including a disability sport curriculum within a PE program is that it can involve reverse mainstreaming whereby students without disabilities play a sport designed specifically for those with disabilities. This not only promotes sports for those with disabilities, but also levels the playing field, because students without disabilities often need to learn new skills. In addition to shooting and dribbling skills, wheelchair basketball requires chair skills that many students who do not use wheelchairs do not possess.

Changing or Modifying Activities Using the STEPS Process

The STEPS process can help teachers change or modify activities along the inclusion spectrum by considering the student (S), the tasks (T), the equipment (E), personnel (P), and safety (S) (see sidebar on page 24). The original acronym, STEP, stood for space, task, equipment, and people (Cereijo Roibas, Stamatakis, & Black, 2011). The version proposed here uses *student* rather than *space* and *personnel* rather than *people* and adds a safety component. Personnel, particularly those involved with the collaborative team, are essential to successful participation. The STEPS process is particularly useful with modified activities on the inclusion spectrum because it helps teachers address appropriate skills across a range of activities.

Conclusion

Teaching is an art that requires much trial and error to get it just right. When using the inclusion spectrum, physical educators must consider the class, the skill they are teaching, and the skills of the student with ASD. Careful planning, appropriate equipment, and an analysis of the curriculum are essential for creating an inviting environment in which students feel safe and supported, one that encourages active participation. In very simple terms, the goal is to keep *all* students smiling and sweating!

STEPS Process

S = Student. Knowledge of the student's skills and abilities is helpful in developing lessons and creating teams. The IEP provides useful information about the student's disability and how it affects learning. Related service providers such as occupational, speech, and physical therapists may have valuable input that can provide a complete picture.

T = Tasks. Once the initial lesson tasks have been established, the teacher can modify them according to the skills and abilities of the student. Modifications can include the number of completed tasks, how the task is performed, and the amount of time taken with each task or the number of required repetitions. The teacher or the students themselves can provide modifications; however, the focus should remain on the student's successful completion of the tasks.

E = Equipment. Proper equipment is essential. Providing a large variety of equipment and allowing students a choice gives students the opportunity to select the equipment best suited to their skills and ability levels. When purchasing equipment, schools should make sure that everyone in the class can have his or her own piece of equipment. This maximizes the opportunities to respond and reduces wait time. Many companies offer specialized equipment suited to a variety of skill levels and performance abilities.

P = Personnel. When teachers are developing lessons, they need to consider how much peer and paraprofessional support they will need. Can classmates support the learning of a student with ASD? In the case of a student with behavioral issues, it is preferable to have the paraprofessional work with the group to monitor behaviors. The physical education teacher is responsible for instructing the paraprofessional in how best to support the student with ASD.

S = Safety. Attention must be given to students' personal behaviors and physical safety when creating lessons. Some types of equipment can trigger negative behaviors, and games can result in overstimulation, which can lead to perseverations. Spatial issues are a concern as well. Teachers need to set clear boundaries and reiterate the need to give everyone personal space as needed.

Proactive Strategies for Inclusion

Ann Griffin, Michelle Grenier, and Pat Yeaton

• •

David, a third-grader, exhibited characteristics similar to those of others on the autism spectrum. Identified as having Asperger syndrome, he had difficulties with many social skills such as reading facial cues and understanding another point of view. Attending physical education (PE) made him anxious, and he was easily flustered by the unpredictable and sometimes chaotic events in the gymnasium. For example, at the beginning of class, when students were completing their warm-up laps around the gymnasium, David would get upset and cry when students passed him as he was jogging. Other events, such as taking turns and sharing equipment, would frustrate him to the point that he would literally curl up in a ball and cry.

When talking with others, David spoke loudly making it seem as if he were angry. His attempts at communicating were not always socially desirable, nor were they clearly understood. Often, his reactions to events caused the students to say, "Oh, that's just David. He always acts that way when he gets mad."

Because Ms. Evans had been David's physical education teacher for four years, she understood what he could do and was sensitive to his needs. Despite this, she believed that her class created a level of anxiety that both frustrated him emotionally and challenged him physically. David indicated this with his body language. Every time he entered the gymnasium, he scowled and shuffled his feet as if it were the last place he wanted to be. While his peers stood on the line waiting for directions, David would lie facedown with one hand under his head pretending to be asleep. His reluctance to engage in the class activities made it difficult for him to have positive relationships with his peers.

To increase David's chances of successfully participating in the class, Ms. Evans created two social stories that addressed specific disruptive behaviors (Gray, 2000). The first described how David could jog safely around the gym, and the other explained the proper procedure for getting a drink at the water fountain during class breaks. Ms. Evans found that David came to rely on these social stories to help him feel more comfortable in the gymnasium. Throughout the year she created several other social stories, depending on the challenges that arose for David.

• •

As noted in the opening scenario, being proactive helped Ms. Evans plan for success by anticipating potential problems and carefully considering the needs of her student with autism spectrum disorder (ASD). The foundation for planning begins with understanding common challenges students with ASD experience, such as difficulty communicating and transitioning and uneven developmental rates, which may significantly affect their success in physical education.

The first part of this chapter describes some common behavior issues students with ASD face. The second part describes innovative teaching strategies and assistive technologies that can be used to address these issues. Assistive technologies addressed include the iPad, social stories, visual scripts, and video modeling. When combined with the practice of previewing, these resources can help teachers create a wrap-around effect whereby students learn from multiple sources (Grenier & Yeaton, 2011). The chapter concludes with an overview of applied behavior analysis (ABA) and how this intervention model can be used within a structured teaching environment.

Communication

Many students with ASD have trouble understanding spoken language. Some are very literal in their interpretation of language and, as a result, need a longer response time during conversations. In other words, students with ASD may be delayed in both expressive and receptive language. Taking turns speaking during conversations and working with others may be difficult because of delayed learning in understanding facial expressions and emotions. Some students are also nonverbal. Following are general recommendations and strategies to better communicate with students with ASD.

• **Determine the communication style of the student.** Special education teachers, speech language pathologists, and paraprofessionals can provide support in this area. Use symbols from Boardmaker, an iPad, or another communication device.

• **Communicate class expectations on a daily basis, and present information visually.** Options include visual planners or a daily schedule, a whiteboard, or picture cues. Preview physical education with the paraprofessional or teacher to let students know what to expect.

• **Offer visual cues.** Modeling is an effective visual instructional and communication technique. Task cards, photos, and videos can also provide clear information. Task cards are helpful for all students and adult assistants in the gym. Many pieces of equipment have picture cues to help students understand them.

• **Give short, precise directions that are positively stated, telling the student what to do rather than what not to do.** For example, use the directive "Walk" rather than the phrase "Don't run."

• **Give direction with statements, *not* questions.** Do not pose a question if you are not offering the student options. Rather than say, "Are you ready to run your laps?" try, "It's time to run; would you like to do two laps or three?" and then begin moving.

• **Give directions in a low, firm voice.** Do not yell or shout. Do not overexplain or repeat the direction over and over. State the direction and wait. Equipment or activity choice boards can be easily made using photos from equipment catalogs. Say, "We are playing catch today. Which ball do you want to use?" Giving students choices helps to engage them in the activity.

• **Pay attention to nonverbal communication.** The ability to use expressive language or to speak coherently is not indicative of cognitive ability. Many students who are nonverbal are very bright. Try to appreciate what students are trying to tell you with their gestures. For example, students who are nonverbal may communicate by pulling you to a specific location.

• **Minimize sport jargon, which can be very confusing.** Students with ASD tend to be rather literal in their interpretation of language and may do exactly what you say. For example, if you say, "Fingers on the laces," the student may touch her shoelaces rather than the laces on the football. "Run home" may be misinterpreted as a directive to literally run to their home. If you say, "Keep your eye on the ball," the student may touch his eye to the ball. "Gallop back" may be taken to mean gallop backward rather than back to a place in line. Some students confuse *gym*

Communication cards made from Boardmaker (a software program used in schools).

with *Jim*, thinking that is their physical education teacher's name.

Social Participation

Many students with ASD have difficulty understanding social situations, which makes having friends or working in groups challenging. Difficulty understanding socially appropriate behavior may cause students to stand too close to others or obsess verbally on a particular topic of interest such as trains or historical figures. Some students become attached to a particular piece of equipment or activity. Others do not have very good eye contact and may not know how to approach social situations. These issues can be likened to an iceberg: although certain problematic behaviors are visible, the underlying causes (below the surface) may be an inability to amuse oneself, poor interactions with peers, and loneliness during unstructured times.

At the core of the behaviors of students with ASD are social skill deficits. Physical educators need to keep in mind that these students may not understand the concept of rules and may need instruction in equipment use. For example, what may seem like a simple chasing and fleeing game may require specific instruction on how to

tag, stay within the boundaries, and change roles.

Physical education teachers must establish a trusting relationship with their students with ASD by working hard to understand how they communicate. The more students feel comfortable with their teachers, the more they are apt to respond to their requests. Alternatively, the more teachers get to know these students, the better they will be at understanding their actions and behaviors.

Physical education is a great environment in which to teach, reinforce, and help students practice social skills. Teachers should examine the student's IEP goals and try and incorporate any specifically intended to enhance social interaction and participation in PE. Simply including a student in PE may not be productive without specifically addressing the social behaviors identified in the IEP. See figure 4.1 for a list of suggestions for addressing social participation.

Uneven Developmental Rates

Many students with ASD have awkward movement patterns and a great variability in gross motor skills (Donnellan, Leary, & Robledo, 2006). For example, a student who likes to run around the gymnasium during the warm-up part of the class may not be able to strike a ball with a racket. The

Social Participation Recommendations

- Explain what it means to have ASD to the student's peers or you can use disability awareness activities. There are many books, DVDs, and online resources that can help you explain the disorder to the students. Developing empathy and understanding are central to encouraging relationships among students.

- Finding a partner can be stressful for students with ASD, so teach them how to find a partner or how to change partners. The direction "Get a partner" does not specifically tell the student what to do. Plan a specific strategy to use when directions are given. For example, tell the student, "When I say 'Get a partner,' look for Luke and Abby." Partners can be arranged in numerous ways that don't isolate the student.

- Teach turn taking. Strategies include changing roles after a certain number of repetitions and using a timer or music.

- Use peers as role models. Reinforce demonstrations of positive social interactions in physical education, as in, "Heidi and Tony, nice job taking turns on the stair stepper."

- Create social stories to help students with particular issues such as changing in the locker room or working with different people. The goal of a social story is not to change behavior, but to teach an understanding of the situation, including the perspective of the social partner.

FIGURE 4.1   For students to be successful in PE, teachers must address their social participation skills.

first task requires only a locomotor pattern, but the second is much more complex. As a result, the student may exhibit behaviors that reflect anxiety about performing the skill. Much will depend on students' familiarity with the equipment and what they are being asked to do. Physical educators should expect a wide range of skill levels in any given student.

Because what works for some students with ASD may not always work for others, teachers need to be flexible about what it means to be actively engaged. For example, a fitness ball may be used as a seat for a student who has trouble standing in place while listening to directions. This enables him to work on bouncing and balancing skills, and if the ball is big enough, to use it as a manipulative for rolling and trapping. Repeating activities can be helpful because familiarity with the task helps the student focus on practicing the skill. It can also help other class members whose skills may be poor.

Restricted Repertoire of Interests

A student with ASD can be drawn to a specific ball, items of a particular color or texture, or an activity. Features of the equipment such as black holes, strings, or spinning parts may attract attention. Physical educators can use this interest to broaden students' repertoire of skills. If a student loves puzzles, for example, the teacher could create a poly spot skeleton puzzle to forge a relationship with the student. Students who love to match colors can be given a five-gallon bucket of beanbags of various colors and be asked to sort them by throwing. A student who likes to line things up can be asked to line up equipment by size, shape, or color. Having gotten the student's attention, the teacher can then try to expand the student's interest by showing her other things to do with the equipment (e.g., move the puzzle pieces farther away or toss or slide the beanbags, stack them, or balance them on body parts).

Capitalizing on student interest can also be an opportunity to build flexibility by teaching skills in a variety of settings. Generalization will need to be planned in different settings by the teacher as it is difficult for students with ASD to transfer skills from one setting to another without specific planning that can naturally embed learned skills. Teaching a parachute activity outside after using it in the gymnasium helps the student generalize from one setting to the next.

Transitions

Transitions, such as going from the classroom to the gym or starting and stopping activities, can be challenging for students with ASD. To help them deal with change, physical educators can use signals such as timers or music to indicate that a change is going to occur. Visual or auditory signals such as timers on cell phones or iPad applications are good choices. Such signals can go a long way in alleviating anxiety or avoiding tantrums. Predictable routines are very helpful in minimizing the stress students with ASD might experience in the gymnasium. Only after a routine is established should aspects of the class be changed.

Assistive Technology

Assistive technology (AT) supports daily tasks such as moving around and communicating. AT can be as simple as an adapted piece of equipment or an image illustrating a particular skill. It can also be quite complicated given the many applications and communication devices available to augment verbal communication.

iPad Applications

iPad applications using writing, drawing, gestural systems, objects, and pictures are the most recent trend to hit the market. Applications on the iPad's touch screen help students with expressive communication, identify feelings, and point to images that convey intent. In most cases, the student knows what to expect when he taps a picture through direct visual contact. Certain applications may be more relevant than others depending on the teacher's goal and how the graphics match to words or actions. The iPad is also useful for reviewing skills on a screen. Watching a breakdown of a throwing skill can help students with ASD understand how to perform the skill and what will happen when they attempt it. Teachers need to keep in mind, too, that different applications work best for different students.

Because iPads are much more portable than computers or other communication devices, they are easy to incorporate into the gymnasium. They can be positioned at a station to model exercises or skills, or they may accompany the paraprofessional or speech therapist to facilitate transitions between activities. The layout of the iPad makes it accessible for students who find tapping easier than typing. Because it is easily carried, it may help calm and focus students who are moving between school environments (www.squidoo.com/iPad-for-autism). Following are some of the most popular applications:

- *Proloquo2Go* brings text-to-speech voice, symbols, and a vocabulary of over 7,000 items to the iPad, iPhone, or iPod touch.

- *ChoiceBoard-Creator* reinforces appropriate choice by expanding the selected image with associated auditory rewards.

- *Dance Party Zoo* uses a dancing game to help students develop basic motor and balance skills.

- *Picture Planner* is a day or event planner that uses images with prompts and reminders to help people stay on track. Totally customizable and mobile, Picture Planner is viewable on the iPad and iPod touch. Schedules can be synched to a computer or mobile device.

- *TouchChat* is a platform for developing vocabulary for people who have difficulty using their own voice. It works amazingly for students on the autism spectrum with emerging language ability. It is flexible, intuitive, and powerful.

It can be overwhelming to sort through the applications available for iPads. For more information and a list of applications that can be used for the iPad, go to www.autismspeaks.org/family-services/autism-apps.

Graphic Organizers

Graphic organizers can provide a structure for learning skills, activities, and games by displaying and arranging the tasks to be accomplished. One of the most common types of graphic organizers is the pictorial schedule, which can outline the events of the class and help students with ASD transition between activities (Waugh, Bowers, & French, 2007). In figure 4.2, images are arranged horizontally and the tasks are arranged vertically. Fittipaldi-Wert and Mowling (2009) also suggest using the Picture Exchange Communication System (PECS), which includes individual cards or symbols that are used to communicate any number of events including the daily schedule, an activity station, or a specific skill. Boardmaker, a software program used in schools by many teachers and therapists, includes thousands of pictures and symbols that can be uploaded to templates used to develop graphic organizers (www.mayer-johnson.com/boardmaker-software).

Simplicity is the key when developing a graphic organizer. There should be as little text as possible, and it should be no more than one page in length. When developing organizers, teachers can photograph students performing a skill or find skills online or in a resource textbook (see figure 4.3 for an example).

Social Stories

Social stories provide meaningful accounts of potentially challenging situations in order to focus and guide students' thinking. Because many students have difficulty with norms and expected behaviors, stories script out what can happen and how they should respond (Gray, 2000). Unlike graphic organizers that outline skills or events, social stories help students with ASD understand common nuances that many students without ASD pick up through social interactions. The following blog has helpful hints on writing a social story: http://blog.autismspectrumdirectory.com/2011/01/29/step-by-step-instructions-how-to-write-a-social-story. When developing social stories, teachers should write the story in the first person as Ms. Evans did with David. The story should include a description of the student's behavior and end with a description of the desired behavior. Pictures can be used to represent the desired actions. Many online ready-made social stories can be accessed through the Gray Center (www.thegraycenter.org/social-stories/how-to-write-social-stories).

Initially, physical educators should read the story with the student to ensure that she comprehends the message. It is helpful to have the student read the story aloud so the teacher can answer any questions the student may have. Once the student has grasped the behavior, the frequency of readings can be reduced. When new behaviors emerge, other stories can be created to help the student cope with the triggering situation.

Issues that can be addressed using social stories include lining up, following class rules, getting

Visual Supporters for Supporting Play at Recess

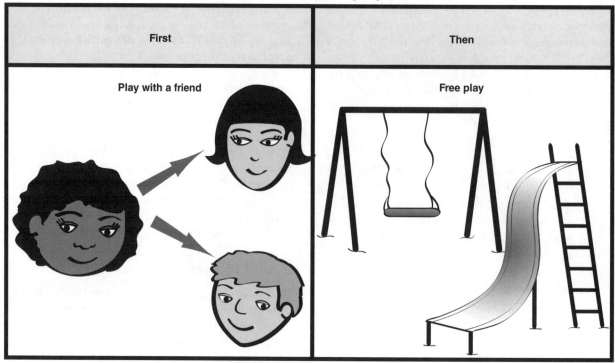

First	Then
Play with a friend	Free play

Friend Choice Board

	I want to play with

FIGURE 4.2 A pictorial schedule can help students with play at recess.

Reprinted by permission from Elizabeth Delsandro.

Grade 3 Ball-Handling Skills

Dribbling With the Hands

___1. Dribble and jog: Dribble in your team area changing directions, pathways, and speeds. Switch the hand that you dribble with. Use many different ways of moving (skip, gallop, sidestep, and walking backward).

___2. Line dribble: Find a line on the floor and dribble and follow your floor lines in any direction. If you meet someone, pass each other right shoulder to right shoulder and dribble with your left hand.

___3. Hoop relay: Have your equipment manager place four hoops on the floor 2 feet (60 cm) apart. The team lines up in front of the first hoop, and the first player zigzag dribbles around the hoops. At the last hoop, dribble inside the hoop five times and dribble straight back passing the ball to the next person in line. Do this until everyone on the team has had two turns.

___4. Dribble tag: Everyone is dribbling and trying to protect the ball. Try to flick the ball from one of the other players. Remember to watch where you are going, and stay in your team area! If you tap another person's ball, you get a point. Play until someone on your team gets 5 points.

FIGURE 4.3 A visual lesson plan is a type of graphic organizer that helps students with ASD transition between activities.

a drink of water, working with a partner, working on a team, and choosing partners. Physical education teachers can collaborate with others who are familiar with the student in writing the story. Pat Yeaton, coauthor of chapter 8, shares examples of social stories used to support David in the beginning scenario.

> **Doing Laps.** Usually when we go to PE class, Ms. Evans has us line up on the black line. Then, we jog around the gym. Ms. Evans likes it when we don't pass each other. Sometimes kids pass me when we are jogging, and I don't like that. When I get mad, I need to remember that Ms. Evans will deal with the kids who are not following the rules.

> **Taking a 1-2-3 Drink.** Usually when we are done jogging for two minutes, we get a drink of water at the fountain in the gym. Ms. Evans likes it when we take quick, 1-2-3 drinks. Sometimes kids take longer than a 1-2-3 count for drinks. When I get upset that they are taking longer drinks, I need to remember that Ms. Evans will speak to the kids who are taking too long.

Previewing

One of the primary goals of previewing is to present social stories or graphic organizers that can reduce the anxiety experienced by students with ASD. Social stories and graphic organizers can be previewed before a student's arrival to the class (Grenier & Yeaton, 2011). Giving the occupational therapist or a student's paraprofessional a copy of a visual lesson plan can help that person familiarize both the student and the paraprofessional with upcoming events in the gymnasium. Depending on the needs of the student, previewing can occur in either a large-group setting such as the classroom, or in a smaller, more focused setting such as the occupational therapist's room. PE teachers can also preview skills to an entire class in the hallway before they entire the gymnasium. This not only helps the student with ASD, but also reinforces learning outcomes with other class members.

Multiple previewing opportunities help students understand that everyone is on the same page, with the same expectations and assumptions for learning (Wallin, 2009). In the long run, these successes encourage students to monitor their own behavior by promoting independence and self-reliance.

When previewing a specific skill, such as striking, the occupational therapist can use a graphic organizer to break down the skill and focus on the learning cues such as stepping with the opposite foot when throwing or having ready hands when catching. Social stories can be presented to a student while entering the gymnasium, or a paraprofessional may read it with the student at any time during the day. Social stories may be combined with graphic organizers to support visual learning through multiple avenues.

Video Modeling

Video modeling (i.e., watching videos of other students or teachers demonstrating the sequence of motor skills) can be a very effective tool for helping students with ASD understand complex skills, particularly when they can practice them prior to the start of class. Research on children with ASD has shown that video modeling can greatly improve social interaction skills, communication skills, play skills, and perceptions of emotions (Rayner, Denholm, & Sigafoos, 2009). Video modeling can also be used to teach social interaction behaviors such as making appropriate comments during a game, as well as to provide perspective on the behaviors of others (Charlop-Christy & Daneshvar, 2003).

Types of video modeling include basic video modeling (VM), video self-modeling (VSM), point-of-view video modeling (PVM), and video prompting (VP) (Banda, Copple, Koul, Sancibrian, & Bogschutz, 2010). Basic video modeling involves viewing someone else engage in the targeted skill or behavior. The student watches the video prior to the instruction or application of the targeted behavior. The desired skill should be highlighted in the video so the student can follow the game pattern or sequence. In video self-modeling the learner is the model in the video. Point-of-view video modeling involves highlighting elements of the environment or activity from the vantage point of the student who needs to acquire the targeted behaviors. The videographer records steps from one setting to another at the eye level of the student. Students watching the video see exactly what they will see when they perform the task, from beginning to end. Point-of-view video modeling increases familiarity with the settings and provides a picture of the completed process, which can reduce anxiety and inappropriate behavior. Lastly, video prompting is done by breaking the skill down into steps (task analysis) and recording each one separately.

Video modeling is particularly effective when it is done with either the occupational or physical therapist at a time when key aspects of the skill can be highlighted and reinforced. Students can also view quick snippets of the video prior to entering the gymnasium or view the skill during the class on an iPad, if available. Because so many students are screen driven, this can be an effective way to capture and maintain a student's attention during the class.

A collaborative model is necessary for working with occupational and physical therapists. What this essentially means is that the physical or adapted physical education teacher needs to establish a positive relationship with the learning team members who work most directly with the student. A collaborative model provides consistency in delivering instruction and services at a number of levels. See figure 4.4 for a description of the video modeling process.

Applied Behavior Analysis

Applied behavior analysis (ABA) has been used for decades because of its demonstrated success with students with ASD. It is based on the traditional theory of behaviorism, focusing on the functional relationship of behaviors to the environment and specifically designed techniques to bring about positive changes in behaviors (www.autismspeaks.org/what-autism/treatment/applied-behavior-analysis-aba). It is a "systematic arrangement of consequences to alter a person's response (or at least frequency of response)" (Loovis, 2011, p. 102). For a student with ASD it could mean defining the elements of the skills of, or the tasks involved in, throwing and catching.

ABA operates under the premise that the environment has a significant impact on behavior through the use of stimuli and reinforcements. A stimulus influences behavior, whereas a reinforcer increases or maintains the student's response to the stimulus. Other common terminology asso-

ciated with ABA are *positive and negative reinforcement, antecedents* (events that occur before a behavior), and *extinction* (the elimination of a behavior).

ABA techniques involve a variety of procedures that are initiated by either the instructor or the learner. Positive reinforcements for demonstrating socially acceptable behaviors are provided in both planned and unstructured environments. Social and natural reinforcers operate as strong reinforcers. Reinforcers are categorized as primary reinforcers (stimuli that address biological needs), secondary reinforcers (e.g., praise, grades, and reward systems), and a system that makes use of the Premack principle. This principle states that a person will perform a less-than-desirable activity to have an opportunity to perform a desired activity. The Premack principle is especially useful in getting students to do things they would rather not do, although teachers need to know what activities they like. If students are engaged in relevant curricula, social and natural reinforcement may be all that is needed.

Students with ASD are strong visual learners and are quick to pick up patterns and routines. Setting up a structured teaching environment supported by ABA facilitates student understanding and helps to decrease negative behaviors (Mesibov, Shea, & Schopler, 2004). It uses student strengths in visual understanding and memory to organize the learning environment so students can understand what is expected. In physical education, structured teaching can easily be applied. Educators can set up the gym so that students can tell where they should be and what they should do. Taking a careful look at the gymnasium or teaching space with a keen eye toward creating a structured physical environment can encourage the participation of students with particular sensory issues. See table 4.1 for ideas on structuring the environment.

Conclusion

Although there are many commonalities among students with ASD overall, differences among individual students can be great. For this reason, physical educators need to get to know each student to understand his or her unique differences. Careful planning and collaboration with other educators will help ensure success with strategies such as graphic organizers and social stories. Even

Video Modeling Process

Preplanning for Video Modeling

1. Written physical education lesson plans are prepared and given to the OTs and PTs one week prior to the lesson being taught.

2. Skills, activities, and lessons are videoed prior to the student's lesson and downloaded onto the school network.

3. OTs and PTs preview the lesson plan and video with students receiving their services prior to their participation in the PE class. OTs and PTs can modify the viewing as per the needs of the student (with or without audio, pausing video to replay portions to reinforce, pausing to practice the skill or activity). OTs and PTs hear the language the PE teacher uses for cues and use that same language when teaching to reinforce the learning. Upon completion of the preview, the student then practices the skills and activities with the OT or PT.

4. OTs and PTs preview, preteach, and practice the lesson with the students to help foster their success and confidence in the PE classroom and outside.

5. OTs or PTs decide whether to continue previewing or just practice the skill.

6. The PE teacher or the PT or OT also recommends other students who may benefit from this learning option. The OT or PT then can invite other students or buddies to preview and practice with them as well.

Making the Video

- When making videos, use young adults who can demonstrate the skills and activities as well as the students' peers individually and in small or large groups. The most beneficial seems to be a small group of students.

- When videoing skills that require more than one person, use only the required number of people to replicate the skill.

- When videoing complex skills, make sure the preliminary work has been done at the fundamental levels of skill development.

Benefits of Video Previewing

- Students come into class with a better understanding of what is being presented.

- Students arrive to class knowing what the lesson is and can anticipate what is coming next.

- Students are more confident in their participation.

- Students are more confidently able to act as models and demonstrate a skill or activity that the teacher is presenting to the class. As with any students, it is great to see students with ASD have peers look up to them to learn something whether it is how to perform a skill or how to participate in an activity.

- The fact that the PE teacher, OT, and PT use the same language when teaching helps reinforce the skill or activity.

- Students have a variety of learning styles presented to them prior to class participation—audio, visual, kinesthetic—in a one-on-one setting with plenty of time to explore and practice.

Feedback From PE Teacher, OT, PT, and Parents

- Feedback about the impact of video modeling reveals that it increases self-confidence and participation in PE and extends to behavior outside the classroom.

- Students look forward to the preview and practice.

- Some of our students call it the PE channel. One of our parents told us that when their child gets on the computer, he asks to go to YouTube and look up exercise (e.g., jumping jacks) and watches them and practices.

- We do not limit this to PE lessons. OTs and PTs also work with skills students use in after-school activities (e.g., running, jump rope).

FIGURE 4.4 The PE teacher needs to work with occupational or physical therapists (or both). This is a model that works for one PE teacher.

Courtesy of Nancy Miller–Newmarket Elementary School, Newmarket, NH.

TABLE 4.1 Structuring the Environment

Areas to improve	Structuring suggestions
Environment	Divide the gym space into activity areas that are clearly defined: walking on river rocks, exercising on mats, cup stacking on tables.
	The physical size of the gymnasium may cause problems. Begin instruction in a smaller setting: classroom, wrestling room, area within a multipurpose room. Provide small spaces in which students feel secure, such as pop-up cubes, tents, or tunnels.
	Most gymnasiums have multiple doors (exits, entrances, locker room doors, equipment room doors, concession area doors, bathroom doors). Think carefully about maintaining a safe environment. Secure doors to keep students safe and in the vicinity of instruction. Know whether you have "runners," and be prepared by planning ahead. Make sure that support personnel have appropriate footwear for the chase, if necessary.
Equipment	Exercise mats let students know where they need to be for warm-up exercises. The mats define the space that each student or set of partners needs to work in.
	Many visual cues commonly used in physical education help clarify the space, task, and activity sequence. These cues are vital for students with ASD, but they also structure the physical education environment for all students. Numbered cones can indicate the sequence of stations or activities. Cones can also be used to hold task cards. Poly spots can easily indicate class formation, foot placement, lines for turn taking, and partner placement. Many are available with numbers, letters, arrows, and exercises. Deck tennis rings can be used to place balls at stations to keep them from rolling away.
	Minimize visual distractions. Keep unnecessary equipment out of sight. Put it away or hide it.
Layout	Setting up activity stations helps students know what to do and where. Bowling stations can be set up using equipment in the gym or commercially available bowling mats. Either setup provides students with lots of visual cues regarding the task.
Lighting	Gymnasium lighting (mercury vapor lights or fluorescent lights) can be problematic. The lights can also cause floor glare, which can be a distraction or a deterrent to participation. Turning off a bank of lights or using natural lighting can help minimize this issue.
Sound	Gymnasium acoustics can also negatively affect instruction. Some students benefit from the use of noise-canceling headphones. Adjusting the volume on the PA system or stereo may also help. Using a signal other than a whistle is another simple modification that can minimize auditory distractions and enhance student engagement.

with excellent planning and instruction, there will be days when nothing seems to work. Teachers need to approach instruction with an open mind and a problem-solving attitude and be flexible and willing to try new things when things don't go as planned.

A variety of iPad applications and videos allow students to watch models of social situations that can help them learn appropriate ways to interact and develop skills. Careful selection of what to use and when will maximize both physical and social skill development.

Reducing Stress to Optimize Learning

Rebecca K. Lytle

• •

Sara is a young teenage girl with autism spectrum disorder (ASD). When she first came to Johnson Middle School, the first unit of physical education was track; then golf. Sara seemed to be doing fine, and in fact, her classroom teacher reported that she was more focused and much calmer immediately after physical education. However, when the unit changed to basketball in the gym, Sara suddenly refused to go to class. After much coaxing, her instructional assistant was able to get her to enter the gym and work a bit on the sidelines with ball skills. However, she was having more trouble in class after physical education and seemed distracted. After consulting with her mother and the occupational therapist, it was discovered that Sara was very sensitive to fluorescent lights and loud noises. The gym lights and echoing sounds of the many basketballs were creating a lot of stress for Sara.

Sara's teachers decided to try a few things to reduce the excessive sensory input for Sara. This included having her wear sunglasses, having her wear earplugs during drill practice when many basketballs were bouncing at once, and letting her take short sensory breaks from the gym every 15 to 20 minutes. Her breaks consisted of simple walks outside in the open air or in a quiet area accompanied by an assistant. These simple methods seemed to help Sara continue to participate in physical education in the gym and also stay focused in the afternoon after returning to class. In fact, the use of the sunglasses for the fluorescent lights and frequent walk breaks were helpful in reducing Sara's stress at other times during the day as well.

• •

Although we may not experience it as acutely as Sara in the opening scenario, we all experience stress, which is defined as any demand on the mind or body. When it results from a positive experience, such as winning a game or having ice cream, it is called eustress. When it results from a negative experience, such as missing a catch or being scared by another's behavior, it is called distress.

For students with ASD, arousal from typical events such as walking to school or talking with friends may vary greatly from that of their peers. In addition to experiencing arousal more intensely and in more situations than their peers, children with ASD may have higher stress levels and take longer to recover from stressful events.

Although no two people are exactly alike, research conducted with people with ASD suggests that variations in the brain (e.g., in the amygdala, the area that perceives threat) may contribute to differences in their responses to events. In addition, in some people with ASD, stress hormones produced by the brain have been found to be at significantly higher levels than those of their typical peers. Moreover, variations in these hormones throughout the day are also greater (Corbett, Mendoza, Abdullah, Wegelin, & Levine, 2006; Jansen et al., 1999; Tani et al., 2005). Parents also express significant concerns about the stress levels of their children with ASD and their ability to cope with environmental demands (Lee, Harrington, Louie, & Newschaffer, 2008). Understanding variations in the stress response and what may trigger added stress for people with ASD can be helpful in planning appropriate programming in physical education settings.

What Is the Stress Response?

When we think of the word *stress,* we often think of negative events as defined earlier as distress. The stress, or distress, response we have to such events is also known as the fight-or-flight response—the feeling we get when we are angry, afraid, or feeling threatened. This feeling is regulated by a series of physiological events, as seen in figure 5.1. However, stress is not inherently bad; it is merely any demand placed on the mind or body. When we perceive something, we simultaneously attach an emotion to that sensation. For example, a light stroke on the arm might feel good to one person, but for the person with ASD, this might be horrible. Thus, the person is fearful of touch. In another example, one person might find solving math problems interesting or challenging and for another, the mere mention of the word *math* creates anxiety. The emotion that goes along with the event and sensation determines whether we perceive it as a positive or negative stressor.

Consider a teacher who is very excited about using the cooperative game Human Knots in her class. She believes that all of the students will succeed because it de-emphasizes competition. For one student, this is very exciting. Young Josh is happy because he does not like competition or having to perform a skill in front of others. He is thrilled that he can relax today during physical education. This game takes the pressure off because it is up to the group to make the game a success. He is also very good at puzzles and logic, so he is happy to play. In contrast, Jaime, who has ASD, does not like to touch other people and likes to have a very large personal space around her. The touch of others often feels like needles on her skin. For Jaime, this activity may create a heightened sense of arousal and anxiety. Clearly, what is pleasant for one student may be highly distressful for another.

Whether a person experiences an activity as stressful can also be related to a sense of control. For Josh, the Human Knots game makes him feel comfortable because it requires skills he is good at and has control over. However, for Jaime, physical touching makes her feel out of control and uncomfortable. A teacher who understands these

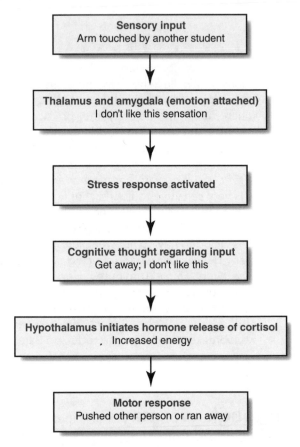

FIGURE 5.1 Example of the stress response in action during a physical education class.

Signs of Stress

- Fidgeting
- Uncontrollable movements such a legs bouncing
- Inability to focus
- Being easily distressed or angry

- Ritualistic or compulsive behavior
- Sleep disturbances
- Memory impairments
- Narrow focus of thinking
- Difficulty being soothed

differences can plan activities to support both students. For example, Jaime might enjoy this activity if the touch component were removed. Using pool noodles or jump ropes to connect students may remove the negative sensory stimuli for Jaime. Other students may also find this a fun variation of this simple game.

Sensory Systems

All of the input we receive comes through our seven senses before it goes to the brain where emotion and judgment are attached to that sensation. Many students with ASD have problems processing sensory information, which can create added stress (Cheung & Siu, 2009; Crane, Goddard, & Pring, 2009; Jasmin et al., 2009). People with ASD have described sensory information as painful (e.g., color hurting their eyes, the sound of a voice hurting their ears, or soap or perfume hurting their nose). For some people, trying to process more than one mode of information at a time can also be overwhelming (Jones, Quigney, & Huws, 2003). Some students with ASD need to close their eyes to talk to the teacher or place their head on the desk to hear what the teacher is saying.

Understanding students' particular sensory needs can give teachers insight into why certain behaviors occur. They can then plan strategies to improve learning through stress reduction. It is important to appreciate that no two people with ASD process information in exactly the same way. Figure 5.2 provides a simple questionnaire that can be helpful in understanding how a student responds to sensory information. For example, a student who is highly sensitive to the sun could wear sunglasses outdoors. A student who is highly distracted by the echoes of the gym can wear earplugs or sound-blocking headphones, perform the activity outside, or work with fewer people. Such strategies may be the difference between tolerating a learning space and having a behavioral meltdown. The next section provides a very brief overview of the sensory systems and examples of how they are used in physical education settings.

Visual. Visual receptor cells are located at the back of the eye in the retina. This system provides information for light and dark, color, edge, size, shape, contrast, depth, whole versus parts, figure-ground, acuity, and movement. Examples in physical education include recognizing numbers and colors, judging size distances for throwing and catching, and maneuvering through a space or among others during an activity.

Auditory. This system is made up of the external ear, middle ear, and inner ear. Receptors for the auditory system are located in the cochlea. This system processes information about sound, pitch, location, timing, intensity, patterns, sound difference, and auditory figure-ground. During physical education class, students need to respond to cues and follow music timing or sequencing. They may also need to process directions or discriminate information from a peer or teacher from the background noise of balls and other activities.

Gustatory. The sense of taste includes, salty, sweet, bitter, and sour. People also sense textures when eating. This system is typically not used during physical activity. However, some students can be calmed by chewing gum for proprioceptive input. This may be possible during walking exercise but is not advisable during other activities because it can be a choking hazard.

Olfactory. Air passes through the nasal canals to the olfactory nerve and then to the brain for interpretation. The sense of smell has a strong connection to memory. Smell can also play a role in the physical education class. For the child who is extrasensitive, the smell of rubber balls or the scent of a sweaty locker room can affect behavior. In some people severe sensitivity can activate the gag reflex in the presence of particular smells.

Tactile. The sense of touch is regulated by cutaneous (skin) receptors. These receptors allow people to locate touch and determine pressure. Simple daily activities such as giving and receiving hugs, wearing clothes, eating a variety of textured foods, and sitting on furniture are all related to the ability to process touch. In physical education, standing in line or touching others in the course of a game can be very distressing for some students with ASD. In an activity such as basketball, having an opponent in one's space or bumping them can be extremely stressful or even painful.

Vestibular. The vestibular system includes the semicircular canals and the otolith organs (the utricle and saccule) of the inner ear. This system provides information about head and body position in space and orientation to horizontal and vertical planes of movement. Standing and balancing independently, riding a bike, walking a balance beam, balancing on an unstable surface such as sand or grass, and turning upside down for a forward roll are all skills that require an effective vestibular system.

Examining Sensory Information

Name_____ Date_____

Vestibular stimulation (movement and gravity information)

		Yes	No
1.	Enjoys heights or elevators		
2.	Prefers more active play		
3.	Rocks while sitting or standing		
4.	Frequently jumps or bounces		
5.	Likes being tossed in the air		
6.	Likes merry-go-rounds or fast rides		
7.	Frequently spins or whirls		
8.	Has no fear of movement or falling		
9.	Craves being rocked, now or as an infant		
10.	Craves wrestling or tumbling activities		
Total			

Tactile stimulation (touch information)

		Yes	No
1.	Has strong preferences for certain food textures		
2.	Likes being cuddled		
3.	Likes using hands for extended periods		
4.	Seeks lots of touch		
5.	Examines or explores objects by putting them into mouth		
6.	Examines or explores objects by touching them		
7.	Hits or bangs head on purpose (now or in past)		
8.	Pinches, bites, or otherwise hurts self		
9.	Frequently rubs, holds, or manipulates objects of a certain texture		
10.	Chews or sucks on nonedibles frequently		
Total			

FIGURE 5.2 This questionnaire can be used by physical educators to determine how a student responds to sensory information. How does the student experience the world through the senses?

Proprioceptive stimulation (deep pressure, vibration, muscle and joint information)

		Yes	No
1.	Seeks crunchy or chewy foods		
2.	Frequently moves quickly and is unable to move slowly from one position or place to another		
3.	Craves tumbling or wrestling		
4.	Frequently gives or requests firm or prolonged hugs		
5.	Likes to be wrapped tightly in sheet or blanket		
6.	Frequently bumps people or objects without apparent reason, but does not seem accidental		
7.	Holds hands or body (or both) in strange positions		
8.	Likes to hide in small and tight spaces		
9.	Bites or chews on nonedibles (e.g., pens, fingernails, hair)		
10.	Enjoys lifting, pushing, or pressure		
Total			

Auditory stimulation (sound and hearing)

		Yes	No
1.	Seeks out toys, activities, or items that make sound		
2.	Craves music		
3.	Likes to study or work with background music or sounds		
4.	Listens to very loud music		
5.	Enjoys loud repetitive sounds such as train equipment		
6.	Likes to hum, whistle, or sing to self		
7.	Is not bothered by loud crowds of people		
8.	Likes repetitive sounds such as clicking a pen or running water		
9.	Becomes stressed in a quiet environment		
10.	Enjoys certain sounds		
Total			

(continued)

FIGURE 5.2 *(continued)*

(continued)

Visual stimulation (sight and light)

		Yes	No
1.	Likes going outdoors on sunny days		
2.	Looks very closely and carefully at pictures or objects		
3.	Resists having eyes covered		
4.	Likes bright or reflecting objects		
5.	Makes riveting eye contact (excessive amount)		
6.	Prefers TV to reading		
7.	Is not bothered by visually busy spaces (e.g., shopping, markets)		
8.	Enjoys bright colors		
9.	Enjoys visual representations over written		
10.	Thinks in visual images		
Total			

Totals: Vestibular:_____   Tactile:_____   Proprioceptive:_____   Auditory:_____   Visual:_____

Plot your results by shading in the blocks in each column to the level of your total score for each category.

10					
9					
8					
7					
6					
5					
4					
3					
2					
1					
	Vestibular	Tactile	Proprioceptive	Auditory	Visual

The higher the score, the more the person enjoys sensory input from that system. The lower the score, the more likely the person is to avoid input from that system.

FIGURE 5.2   *(continued)*

Proprioceptive. Input from muscle spindles and joint receptors tells the body where it is in space, in addition to sensing the direction and velocity of movement, as well as the effort needed to perform a task. The proprioceptive system is in play when picking up a weight or ball, stepping off a low beam, or mirroring a position from a demonstration. This system is also important for all motor skills such as climbing, crawling, rolling, jumping, and manipulating objects.

In summary, the sensory systems must all be in good working order to be successful in the physical education setting. A child who struggles with processing information from any of the sensory systems will experience a detrimental effect on performance. In many people with ASD, multiple sensory systems are affected. Imagine trying to play basketball if your visual, auditory, and tactile systems were not processing correctly. The environment becomes a highly stressful, unpredictable space full of threat because of an inability to judge distance, filter auditory input, or prevent physical contact with others because of poor spatial orientation, poor proprioception (knowing where you are in space), or motor planning.

Stress Reduction Strategies

Stress reduction strategies are important for getting the most out of any learning environment. To learn, a student needs to be in an optimal state of arousal. People with ASD are often either overaroused or underaroused. Thus, the challenge is finding ways to support the nervous system so that an individual can be as close as possible to an optimal state of arousal for learning. For some people with ASD, the time they are in the optimal state of arousal may be only seconds at a time or minutes at a time, while many neurotypical individuals are able to be in a focused state for hours in a day. The challenge is to help the student who is overaroused or underaroused attain a comfortable arousal state and stay there for as long as possible so that focused learning can take place. Each line in figure 5.3 represents a hypothetical person. One is overaroused, one is underaroused, and several float in and out of the optimal state of arousal as the day goes on. Most people float in and out of the optimal state of learning or arousal throughout the day, depending on fatigue, hunger, outside events, and other stress factors.

Stress reduction strategies are not a new idea, and most techniques that work for anyone can also be applied to students with ASD. They include physical activity, meditation or quiet spaces, environmental changes, music, and breaks (Lytle & Todd, 2009). The following section describes several strategies for stress reduction. Although this is not an exhaustive list, it can serve to stimulate ideas that may be appropriate for a given student.

Exercise. Students with ASD can show improved attention to tasks, reduced stereotypic behaviors, and positive responding following exercise bouts. This is a good reason to provide opportunities for exercise every day or several times throughout the day. However, to attain these beneficial effects, exercise must be familiar and sustained; learning a novel skill or trying to

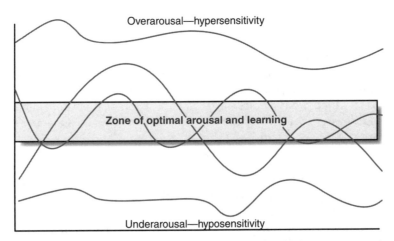

FIGURE 5.3 The zone of optimal arousal represents an arousal level at which a person is relaxed and able to focus and learn. Being too stimulated or not stimulated enough can inhibit the ability to focus.

participate in a complex game or task might have the opposite effect. Walking, jogging, or dancing to music at the beginning of a physical education session can help students with ASD relax and release energy. Taking 15-minute breaks to walk or perform other desired movements (jump on a mini trampoline, swing on swing set, move heavy objects) during the day can also increase students' ability to focus during classroom activities. Depending on the learning environment and the size of the class, the teacher may be able to alternate between having students perform a desired movement task and having them practice a new task. Students can engage in swinging or jumping to calm themselves just before engaging in a more stressful task. In a group instructional setting, teachers may be able to provide a sensory break corner where students can play for a few minutes before returning to the lesson.

Environment. For many people, sensory input from certain lights, sounds, or other stimuli can be bothersome in a learning environment. Because no two people with ASD are alike, understanding each student's sensory needs and stressors is critical to creating a positive learning environment. Working closely with parents, special education teachers, and occupational therapists can be critical in providing appropriate stress reduction strategies. Table 5.1 presents a list of sensory concerns and reduction strategies.

TABLE 5.1 Sensory Concerns and Strategies

Areas of concern	Problems	Strategies
Hypersensitive	Vestibular insecurities; sensitive to smells, lights, sound; pulls away from touch. Signs of stress can include, but are not limited to, shutting down, lacking focus, tantruming, pulling away, acting out, screaming or hitting, exhibiting increased stereotypic behaviors, running away, or being unwilling to participate.	Dim lights, create a quiet environment, limit distractions in the environment, focus on one thing at a time, provide choice. Wear sunglasses or baseball caps to dim glare or fluorescent lighting.
Hyposensitive	Low tone, low affect, bumps into things, craves rough-and-tumble play. Signs of stress can include, but are not limited to, shutting down, lacking focus, tantruming, pulling away, acting out, screaming or hitting, exhibiting increased stereotypic behaviors, running away, or being unwilling to participate.	Colorful environment, high level of activity and movement, music.
Visual	Limited ability to attend to visual input, difficulty following a visual sequence or fixing on a moving object, difficulty discriminating a visual object from a field. Possible signs of stress: blinks, squints, looks out of the corner of the eye, rubs eyes, makes poor eye contact, prefers dark.	Create high contrast of objects to background, reduce the number of visual distractions, use a visual sequence chart, break the whole into small parts, focus on one visual aspect at a time.
Auditory	Difficulty grasping the meanings of words; inability to recall or use words; sound discrimination challenges; trouble detecting pitch, tone, or volume. Possible signs of stress: covers ears, runs away, pulls ears, grinds teeth, makes sounds.	Short, simple directions; visual cues or schedules; rhythm activities; music to create patterns; headphones to reduce noise; calming music.

Areas of concern	Problems	Strategies
Vestibular	Atypical tone; poor balance; poor muscle co-contraction; postural insecurity; disorders of arousal; short attention span; avoidance or seeking of swinging, spinning, twirling. Possible signs of stress: avoids equipment, becomes car sick easily, avoids tilting head, does not like feet off the ground, will not do forward roll.	Provide lots of support for vestibular activities. Ginger tablets can be helpful for those with severe motion sickness. For those seeking vestibular input, swinging can be calming.
Tactile	Tactile defensiveness, tactile seeking behaviors, tactile processing difficulty, hyperactivity or distractibility, poor motor planning. Possible signs of stress: needs large personal space, has an aversion to others, lashes out, is a picky eater, is a picky dresser, does not like busy places.	Deep pressure activities (any activity that puts lots of pressure on the joint receptor) such as moving mats, equipment, and chairs; providing sensory toys to hold or fiddle with during instruction, such as putty or squeeze balls; and, when appropriate, squeezing or body socks.
Proprioceptive	Atypical muscle tone, inadequate muscle contractions for maintaining posture, lack of body awareness, difficulty coordinating movements, difficulty with spatial awareness.	Heavy pushing and pulling activities such as moving heavy things, push-ups, pull-ups, tug-o-war, jumping and landing, weight training—any activities that provide deep pressure to the joints and body. Proprioceptive activities typically have a calming effect and help to reduce stress.

Control. When students have control over their environment, they typically feel safe; for example, at home they know what to expect, know who is there, and can control things such as whether the TV is on. However, a noisy gym crowded with other people is a much more unpredictable environment. Students don't know who will come up and talk to them or what others might do or say, and they typically cannot control the timing, noise level, or sequence of events. Thus, the more teachers can give students a sense of control, the more secure they will feel. Schedules, pictures, routines, preteaching skills, and providing choices can all help to create a more comfortable environment. Choices can be as simple as the type of equipment, size of equipment, number of partners, area to play in, or length of time in an activity. Also, because too many choices can create chaos and discomfort, finding the right balance is important. Often, a choice between two things can help to reduce stress.

Relaxation. There are many types of relaxation techniques. Exercise was previously mentioned and can be an excellent way to reduce cortisol levels and improve relaxation and focus. Other physical activities such as yoga and aerobics can also reduce stress. Yoga can be incorporated into the physical education routine or set up in a corner in the gym. Poses can be posted on the wall, and students can choose to go to the yoga corner when they need a break from the other activities. Another relaxation strategy is a sensory break corner with calming items or sensory toys.

Conclusion

Stress is a part of everyday life and can have a positive or negative influence on behavior. Finding the balance of "just right" stress for people with ASD can be challenging because of the variations in neurological development. Learning what forms of sensory information increase or decrease stress for a student can be one of the secrets to setting up a positive and supportive learning environment and the difference between successful engagement in an activity and a behavioral meltdown.

Assessment and the IEP Process

Martin Block and Andrea Taliaferro

• •

Jorge is a bright-eyed, very active seven-year-old who loves to run, climb, and throw. Anyone watching Jorge play by himself on the playground would never guess that he has any motor or fitness delays. He seems very capable of climbing and sliding down even the highest slide, running around the playground, and throwing mulch from the playground onto the grass. He also seems fairly fit for a seven-year-old with a trim, wiry appearance and an internal engine that never seems to shut off! However, Jorge does not seem as capable when he attends general physical education classes with his second-grade peers. He often stands and watches while his peers run and gallop and slide following musical cues. He likes to run around the gym during tag games, but he does not seem to understand the concept of running away from the tagger. Finally, he does not display good control with ball skills, either kicking or throwing the ball too softly or with too much force to peers. Jorge is a contradiction, but then again, Jorge has autism spectrum disorder (ASD).

Jorge, like many children with ASD, presents a unique challenge to physical educators: how do you determine whether Jorge truly has a motor delay that affects his ability to be successful in general physical education (GPE) or whether his delays are due to behaviors and not understanding what to do? The key to understanding Jorge's strengths and needs is assessment. Assessment will help the general and adapted physical educators determine the underlying cause of Jorge's difficulties in GPE, which in turn will determine whether Jorge qualifies for adapted physical education (APE) services. Once it is determined whether Jorge qualifies for APE, the IEP team will use assessment data to create an appropriate motor program for him. Finally, an assessment will allow the IEP team to determine the most appropriate placement for Jorge with regard to physical education (PE).

• •

This chapter reviews motor, fitness, and sport skill assessment practices for students with ASD, like Jorge in the opening scenario. The chapter begins with specific strategies that will help children with ASD understand what to do and perform at their best. This is followed by a review of assessment tools that might be used with children with ASD. The chapter concludes with information on how to translate assessment data into information that can be used to plan a program and create appropriate IEP goals.

Strategies for Assessing Children With ASD

As noted throughout this book, working with children with ASD presents unique challenges. This is no more evident than when trying to assess a child's motor, fitness, or sport skills. To get accurate assessment data, educators must make sure children with ASD understand what to do and try their best during testing. Following are suggestions for areas to address when testing children with ASD.

Learning About the Child

It is critical that the physical educator learn as much as possible about the child before testing is started. Many children with ASD present unique behaviors, communication issues, and other challenges that require unique testing procedures. Following are some key aspects of the child that may influence how testing is conducted.

Medical background. Before beginning an assessment, the examiner should ask the child's parents or special education teacher about any medical or health issues that might affect testing. For example, a child might be on medication for anxiety that has led to weight gain and lethargy, which would clearly affect fitness testing and general motivation. A complete medical and health history of the child is not necessary; examiners need only information that may influence testing such as the child's energy level and ability to pay attention and focus.

Behaviors. The child's special education teacher or parents, or both, can provide information about any behavior issues that might influence or facilitate testing. For example, it would be helpful to know about particular reinforcers or reinforcement programs that could be used to help the child perform at his best. In contrast, it would be important to know of any triggers that may upset the child so these can be avoided during testing. For example, for a child who does not like loud sounds, balloons in the environment (e.g., to use for a catching exercise) may be scary. Examiners should also be aware of any behaviors that may pose a danger to themselves or the child such as running away or self-injurious or aggressive behavior. Related to this is knowing how to help the child calm down if she does get upset. Again, this type of information is available from the child's special education teacher and parents.

Teaching style. Many children with ASD are under a special teaching system such as applied behavior analysis (ABA) or structured teaching (Treatment and Education of Autistic and Related Communication Handicapped Children [TEACCH]). Whatever system is being used needs to be incorporated into the testing setting. For example, a child in an ABA program will most likely receive reinforcement (token or actual) after a set number of successful trials or a set time period. This system of reinforcement should be used in the gymnasium during assessment. The child would be given a token toward a reinforcer after two minutes (set with an egg timer); then, after receiving a set number of tokens, the child should receive the reinforcer. Similarly, a child in the TEACCH program might be used to having all materials in a basket; when the basket is empty, the child knows she has completed the task. Prior to testing, the physical educator can place all testing materials into a large basket and then take them out during testing. The child can see the basket emptying and know when testing is complete.

Communication. One of the key characteristics of children with ASD is significant deficits in speech and language. With regard to expressive language, some children with ASD can speak, others use picture boards to communicate, and still others use rudimentary forms of sign language. It is important to find out the communication system used by the child and then use this system during testing. It should be noted that most children with ASD understand some verbal language, and most teachers use verbal cues (coupled with other alternative forms of communication) when presenting information. The key is for the physical educator to find out as much as possible about a child's receptive language and how to present information verbally. Many children with ASD get confused when presented with long verbal directions. It may be more appropriate and effective to use a one- or two-word verbal cue (e.g., "Throw") coupled with a gesture such as pointing to the target, rather than saying, "Take your ball and throw it toward the target." The simple command "Jump" coupled with an exaggerated arm swing is better than saying, "Stand on this poly spot, and then when you are ready, swing your arms like I am doing and jump as far as you can" (Payne, Yan, & Block, 2010). Even better would be to show a picture of a child throwing, say "Throw," and then demonstrate throwing.

Preparing the Child for Assessment

A key to a successful, valid assessment session with a child with ASD is preparing the child ahead of time. Children with ASD are easily confused and as a result may become anxious, withdrawn, or agitated. These unwanted behaviors can be avoided by helping the child understand what is going to happen during the testing session. This preparation can be accomplished by using social stories, using schedules, practicing some of the test items in the classroom, and meeting the person who will be conducting the assessment (Payne, Yan, & Block, 2010).

Social stories are very helpful for children with ASD who have strong language skills (e.g., children with Asperger syndrome). The child's teacher or the physical educator writes and then reads (or the child reads) an explanation of what will happen in the upcoming activity, what the child might see, who might be there, and what the expected behaviors are (Sandt, 2008). The following is an example of a piece of a social story for testing:

> Then John [the child's name is usually used in the story] will play a throwing game where he will throw beanbags toward a picture of Kobe Bryant on the wall. There will be lots of beanbags in a bucket. John will pick up the beanbags one at a time and throw as hard as he can at Kobe Bryant. When the bucket is empty, John will be finished with the throwing game.

Finally, an excellent way to prepare a child for testing is to practice some test items in the classroom or the gymnasium. Initially, it is best to practice the test items in the classroom because it is a safe, familiar place for the child. The teacher or teacher assistant can present test items at first, and then later the physical educator can come into the classroom and present others. As the child becomes comfortable with the test items and with the physical educator, he can be brought down to the gym to practice items so he can become comfortable with the testing setting. This does not have to be a long, drawn-out process. Practicing in the classroom can take place three or four times each day for two days; then practicing in the gym can be done two or three times over two or three days.

Conducting the Assessment

As noted earlier, children with ASD often have behavior and communication challenges. These challenges must be addressed to obtain the most valid and reliable assessment results. In other words, physical educators want to make sure they are assessing the child's motor and fitness skills and not her ability to understand directions and stay on task. This section describes how to conduct the assessment in a way that accommodates the child's unique learning needs.

Setting Up the Testing Environment

An important key to successful testing is carefully setting up the environment to make the child as comfortable as possible. The environment should be free of extraneous distractions such as other people and equipment that will not be used during testing. Equipment that will be used during testing should be neatly organized, ideally in the order in which it will be presented to the child. As noted earlier, equipment can be placed in one big basket to cue the child when testing is completed. Or, equipment can be placed in separate baskets relating to each activity. When an activity is complete and the basket is empty, the child will know he is finished with the item. It also may be helpful to allow the child to walk by the equipment so he can see all the things he will do during the testing session. If he is very distractible, it may be useful to keep the equipment for each section of the test hidden until needed. Cones, mats, and other visuals can be used to set up boundaries to define the testing area, particularly if testing is taking place in a large gymnasium. A clearly marked spot such as a poly spot or carpet square should be placed for the child to sit or stand on upon entering the gym. Finally, the child should be allowed to bring a favorite toy or object that he can hold during breaks or sit next to during testing. This may help alleviate anxiety.

Using Visual Schedules

Schedules are often used with children with ASD to help them understand what is expected during the course of a day or a particular period of time. Schedules can be made of words or sentences for children who can read, pictures (photos or drawings) for children who cannot read, or real objects for children who have not learned to identify pictures (Savner & Myles, 2000). In the case of testing, the physical educator (with help from the special education teacher) can create a schedule that explains all the things the child will do during testing. For example, when testing object control skills for the Test of Gross Motor Development-2 (TGMD-2), the teacher might create a picture schedule that includes all the object control skills to be practiced during this session (see figure 6.1).

Using Visual Cues

As discussed previously, students with ASD tend to be visual learners and frequently rely on visual

Tim's Schedule

FIGURE 6.1 Sample picture schedule for TGMD-2.

cues when communicating and trying to understand instructions. Visual cues can be in many forms including demonstrations, photographs, and the Picture Exchange Communication System (PECS). Visual cues are helpful when conducting motor skill assessments. For example, a peer or teacher may demonstrate a skill and then ask the child to imitate it. If the child uses picture cards or PECS to communicate in the classroom or at home, they may be useful during the testing situation as well. The teacher may show the child a photograph of someone performing the overhand throw paired with a short verbal cue. When the child attempts the skill, the teacher offers verbal feedback while showing the child a card with a picture representing the message "Good job."

Another useful visual cue may be in the form of video modeling, in which the child watches a video clip of a model performing the desired skill or behavior and then attempts to imitate the skill. Video modeling has been shown to be an effective strategy in improving play skills, social behaviors, and functional skills in children with ASD (D'Ateno, Mangiapanello, & Taylor, 2003; Delano, 2007; Hine & Wolery, 2006). The video can be of a peer, a teacher, or even the child himself performing the targeted skill or test item. Video modeling can be a useful visual tool in the assessment of motor skills and can be easily watched on a laptop computer, iPad, iPod, or smartphone. The video can be viewed ahead of time at home or in the classroom to prepare the student for the assessment and can be brought to the testing site so the student can watch it prior to each test item to help her understand the expected skill or behavior.

Providing Breaks

Examiners need to consider the time needed to conduct the assessment and determine whether the child can attend to directions, stay on task, and remain motivated for that length of time. One option is to break the assessment into sections and conduct the testing over a period of several days. Another option is to arrange for frequent breaks during testing to allow the child time to rest and transition between activities. For example, after the child performs four test items or remains on task for five minutes, he earns a three-minute break.

Some children with ASD may become overstimulated or agitated by the change in their daily routine, being in an unfamiliar setting, or being asked to follow so many directions during the assessment. For some children with ASD sensory activities help them calm down and regulate their behaviors. If this is the case, a sensory break may be a useful option. For example, a break that includes spinning on a scooter, playing with a favorite sensory object, bouncing on a therapy ball, or listening to calming music might be provided between test items or at specific intervals throughout the assessment.

Testing in Authentic Settings

Information about a student's abilities can also be gathered while the student is engaged in a real-life situation or gamelike activity. This is known as authentic assessment. It is a nonstandardized test that takes place in the student's typical settings, such as in the classroom, on the playground, and during physical education. Authentic assessments often use rubrics or other alternative techniques to gather information on the child's abilities (Block, Lieberman, & Connor-Kuntz, 1998).

Testing in authentic settings may provide more realistic and accurate information than standardized assessments do. Unlike standardized assessments, authentic assessments don't focus on isolated skills in an artificial testing environment or follow strict test guidelines. Instead, students' skills are measured in their traditional environments while they participate in functional tasks that pertain to real-world skills and situations (Block et al., 1998; Siedentop, 1994). For example, running, fleeing, and dodging skills can be assessed while the student is participating in a tag game on the playground. Students' ability to interact appropriately with peers can be observed and assessed while they participate in small-group warm-up activities or large-group cooperative activities in physical education. Appendix 6A presents the University of Virginia Initial Observation and Referral Form, which provides a helpful checklist to use when conducting an authentic assessment.

Testing in authentic settings may be particularly useful when assessing the motor skills of students with more severe ASD who have difficulty following directions or participating in a structured testing environment. In this case, equipment stations or various types of equipment can be set out for the student to choose from and explore in an unstructured manner. As the student engages in play with the equipment, tools such as checklists and rubrics can be used to evaluate general motor abilities.

Popular Assessment Tools in General and Adapted Physical Education

Many standardized assessment tools are appropriate for children with ASD. Following are the keys to choosing one:

- Age of the child (e.g., developmental motor scales for younger children and sport-specific tests for older children)
- Purpose of the assessment (e.g., determining fitness versus motor strengths and weaknesses)
- Ability of the child to understand test directions (Horvat, Block, & Kelly, 2007)

The following assessment categories, taken from Horvat and colleagues (2007), should be considered when testing children with ASD. Assessments are listed in order from tests appropriate for younger children to those for older children.

Developmental Motor Assessment

For children ages two through six, the most appropriate tests are developmental motor assessments. These typically evaluate children's present motor skills compared to age norms. For example, children who follow a normal course of motor development would be expected to jump on two feet by around the age of two, catch a large ball by age three, and walk on a balance beam without stepping off by age four. The typical developmental motor test has several motor tasks listed by the expected age of mastery. For the most part these tests are quantitative, measuring whether a child can perform a particular task (e.g., jumping forward on two feet 24 to 30 in., or 61 to 76 cm) rather than examining the quality of the pattern (i.e., what the jumping pattern looks like). The most popular developmental motor assessment is the Peabody Developmental Motor Scales (PDMS-2) (Folio & Fewell, 2000). These scales present several motor skills in six-month age strands. The age strands represent when most children are expected to have mastered particular skills.

Items found in most developmental motor tests are fairly self-explanatory (e.g., walking up stairs, walking across a balance beam, jumping over a rope, throwing to a target), so most children with ASD should not have too much trouble under-standing what to do. In addition, many items are things they probably have done before (e.g., riding a tricycle, kicking a ball, jumping down from a box). Items targeting older preschool children may require more forceful movements (e.g., jumping farther or kicking so the ball travels farther), and it may be difficult to get some children with ASD to do these forcefully enough to meet the criteria. With these items it is important, although challenging, to make the sure the child focuses on the demonstration and understands the forcefulness needed to be successful.

Fundamental Motor Skill Assessment

As children get older, they begin to develop basic motor patterns including skills such as running, jumping, throwing, and catching. These fundamental motor patterns can be assessed qualitatively to examine how the child performs each skill. These qualitative assessments can be developmental where developmental progressions are presented. For example, when just learning how to throw, children do not step with either foot. As they develop more advanced throwing skills, they progress to first stepping with the same-side foot (e.g., stepping with the right foot when throwing with the right hand) to eventually the most skillful pattern of stepping with the opposite foot. A teacher can evaluate a child's developmental level in throwing and other fundamental motor skills to determine his present level and then determine what to focus on with instruction. Fundamental motor patterns also can be assessed by simply determining whether the child has mastered the mature level of the pattern. For example, in the popular Test of Gross Motor Development-2 (TGMD-2) (Ulrich, 2000), the mature throwing pattern is broken down into the following four components:

1. Initiates windup with a downward movement of the hand or arm.
2. Rotates hips and shoulders so the non-throwing side faces the target.
3. Transfers weight by stepping with the foot opposite the throwing hand.
4. Follows through diagonally across the body toward the nonpreferred side after releasing the ball.

Getting children with ASD to score well on tests of fundamental motor patterns can be a real challenge for the examiner. It is not that the child cannot perform these basic fundamental skills; rather, the problem is getting the child to demonstrate all the components of a mature pattern for each skill. For example, with the two-footed jump, the child is expected to swing the arms back and then forward forcefully (ending with the arms overhead). Although most children with ASD can jump, getting them to understand the concept of swinging their arms forcefully may be difficult. This is true for most fundamental motor patterns (e.g., stepping when throwing, leaping in preparation of a kick). Although there is no easy solution, the best way to help children with ASD understand what to do is to provide a clear demonstration exaggerating key components and setting up the task so that it forces the pattern (e.g., having a target far away to force the child to put more effort into the throw and perhaps demonstrate a step with the opposite foot).

Motor Ability Assessment

Another popular form of assessment is motor ability assessment. Motor ability tests focus on such areas as balance, eye–hand coordination, agility, and dexterity. Items in motor ability tests tend to be novel for children, such as jumping and clapping hands, standing on one foot, performing a shuttle run, or sorting a deck of cards. The advantage of motor ability tests is that they are highly standardized with age norms. Example of popular motor ability tests are the Bruininks-Oseretsky Test of Motor Proficiency (Bruininks & Bruininks, 2005) and the Movement ABC-2 Test (Henderson & Sugden, 2007).

Motor ability tests are perhaps the most challenging type of test for children with ASD. Items tend to be things the child has not attempted (e.g., sorting cards, alternating touching fingers to nose, jumping and clapping). In addition, many items on motor ability tests are timed, requiring the child to move as quickly as possible (e.g., sort cards as quickly as possible, string beads as quickly as possible, perform a shuttle run). Many children with ASD have difficulty (1) understanding exactly what to do and (2) doing the activity quickly enough to score well on these tests. As noted in the earlier section on fundamental motor skill assessment, demonstrations may help the child understand some items, and cheering and clapping might help the child speed up her performance.

Physical Fitness Testing

Physical fitness testing is popular in school settings, beginning in upper elementary grades and continuing through high school. Most physical fitness tests measure strength, flexibility, endurance, and body composition, and most tests have age-normed criteria for what constitutes physical fitness proficiency. For example, in the Fitnessgram (2010), physically fit 10-year-old boys should be able to do 50 sit-ups in one minute, and physically fit 10-year-old girls should be able to do 35 sit-ups in this same time period.

Many students with ASD can participate in fitness testing without modifications to the assessment items. Some, however, require accommodations or alternative test items. When using standardized tests to assess the physical fitness of children with ASD, examiners need to determine whether the children understand the instructions to ensure that the results are a fair representation of their fitness levels. Many physical fitness test items involve multiple-step directions, which may pose a challenge for some students with ASD. For example, in the Fitnessgram (2010) Pacer test, the student must understand where to start and stop as well as how to follow the cadence of the beeps to complete the test successfully. The curl-up test also requires students to understand how to slide their hands the appropriate distance across the testing strip while performing the curl-up motion and follow a recorded cadence at the same time. These multiple-step directions and multiple cues may cause confusion or be overstimulating for students with ASD. In addition, these students may become agitated by the noise and activity around them during fitness testing, particularly if many children are participating in the assessment.

Modifications can be made to physical fitness tests such as the Fitnessgram to allow for the successful participation of students with ASD (Winnick & Short, 1999). General modifications might include testing in a quieter area or room for children who become overstimulated by the noise and activity, or providing a schedule, visual aids such as pictures or video, and multiple demonstrations of the test items to help students understand the directions. Suggestions for modifications to specific test items to encourage and motivate students with ASD are outlined in table 6.1.

It is important to note that if a test has been modified, it may not be appropriate to compare the student's results with the regular standards,

TABLE 6.1   Modifications to Fitnessgram Items

Test	Possible modifications
Pacer	• Place cones or other markers (lines) at the required distance to provide a visual cue of where to start and stop. • Allow the student to run along a line marked on the floor. • Allow the student to run laps without regard to the cadence. • Shorten the distance required. • Allow a peer or instructor to run alongside the student to provide verbal cues such as "Start" and "Stop" and provide demonstrations. • Allow the student to watch others perform the test prior to attempting. • Use additional visual cues such as picture cards or a stop sign to show to the student at appropriate times.
Curl-up cadence	• Allow the student to complete as many curl-ups as possible without following the cadence. • See how many curl-ups the student can perform in a set amount of time (e.g., 1 minute). • Place an object, such as a Koosh ball or beanbag, on the far side of the test strip to give the student a tactile cue when his hands have slid the required distance. Cue the child by saying, "Touch the beanbag." • Instead of using the test strip, allow the student to place her hands on her thighs and slide her hands up to her knees when performing the curl-up. • Place a sticker on the student's knees as a visual cue and ask him to touch the sticker to promote the proper form.
Sit and reach	• Place colored pieces of tape at various distances on the measurement board or the student's leg, and use short verbal cues to ask the student to reach for different colors (e.g., "Touch green"). • Have a peer demonstrate alongside the student. • Provide a footprint or other marker to help the student identify where the feet should be placed.
Push-up	• Allow the student to perform modified push-ups (wall push-ups, knee push-ups). • Allow the student to perform a static push-up. Have the student get into a correct push-up position with elbows extended and body straight. Time how long the student can hold this position. • Use handprints or other markings to help the student understand where to place her hands. • Place an object under the student's chest, such as a book, mat, or ball, and instruct him to bend his arms and lower his chest to touch the object to promote a proper 90-degree elbow angle.
Mile run	• Place buckets or hula hoops at certain distances around the track or running area. Give the student a beanbag and have him run and place it in the next bucket. Have him continue until he has completed the distance. • Allow the student to run a shorter distance (1/4 or 1/2 mile, or 0.4 or 0.8 km) instead. • Have a peer run alongside the student to provide encouragement and verbal cues.

and age-related norms and scores should not be entered into the fitness test software or included in school reports of fitness measures (Silliman-French, Buswell, & French, 2008). However, information gathered from this testing will be useful in determining appropriate fitness goals and provide a baseline for measuring improvements over time.

Sport and Lifetime Leisure Skill Testing

As children reach middle and high school age, the most appropriate tests focus on their ability to perform sport and lifetime leisure skills. Consider tennis. An assessment of forehand, backhand, serve, and volley skills might be qualitative (i.e., what the skill looks like) and quantitative (e.g., how many times the ball goes over the net and into the court). An assessment provides a glimpse of the child's present level in tennis skills and helps the physical educator know what to focus on during instruction. Unfortunately, only one series of standardized sport and leisure skill tests is currently available. Special Olympics (2011) offers skill tests in all the sports it offers. Following is the Special Olympics forehand tennis strike assessment:

1. Athletes turn shoulders and hips to face sideways to the net (racket is in a volley position with the strings facing the net). Use the key words, "stand sideways with your racket back and look like a surfer" or "turn your shoulders."

2. Athletes take the racket back and down (pointing at the back fence and down toward the court surface). The shape of the swing, when put together as one motion, will be a "C" loop.

3. Before initiating the swing, the athlete takes a few adjusting steps toward the ball.

4. Demonstrate the contact point position (freeze this position and emphasize that this is where the ball is contacted).

5. The stroke continues with a balanced follow-through with the racket high and out in front (be careful not to exaggerate the follow-through as athletes will put it all together when actually striking a ball),

racket pointing up and towards the net (like "shaking hands with a giant").

The challenges noted with fundamental motor skills will be an issue when attempting to test sport skills in children with ASD. In particular, children may be able to perform the basic pattern of the skill (e.g., hits a baseball, swings a golf club, or serves a volleyball); however, many children with ASD will not understand the power needed for performing these and similar skills with enough force to be truly successful. For example, performing an underhand serve in volleyball is something most children with ASD are capable of doing, but many will have difficulty serving the ball over the net from a regulation distance. Children who cannot serve from a regulation distance will not be able to play in regular community sport leagues. Again, the key when testing children with ASD is to provide a good demonstration that exaggerates key components and the force needed to be successful.

Alternative Assessments

In some instances, alternative assessments are used instead of or in combination with formal standardized assessments to gather additional information regarding the child's abilities. Such assessments can be used to evaluate students' abilities in the cognitive, psychomotor, affective, and health-related fitness domains. Alternative assessments are often in the form of rubrics or checklists focusing on skills addressed in the general physical education curriculum or on individual student goals. Rubrics consist of a skill or behavior broken down into measurable and observable components (Block, Lieberman, & Connor-Kuntz, 1998).

Teachers can make their own alternative assessments to target particular skills they are interested in, or they may opt to use already existing rubrics. For example, a teacher may select an existing rubric from the curriculum or from a portion of a standardized assessment such as the overhand throw subtest of the Test of Gross Motor Development-2 (it is considered alternative because only a portion of the standardized test is used). Sample rubrics that can be used to evaluate the behaviors and skills of students with ASD can be found in appendix 6B.

Translating Assessment Results Into the IEP

Once testing is complete, it is time to translate the results into a written report including a present level of performance, which will guide the creation of IEP goals and objectives. The first step is to interpret the test results to determine the child's strengths and weaknesses, whether the child is significantly delayed, and possible goals and objectives to target for instruction. Appendix 6C presents a sample assessment report based on the Test of Gross Motor Development-2. In this report, the student (BT) demonstrated the basic object control skills of throwing, catching, and kicking as well as the locomotor skills of running, jumping, and galloping. However, he was missing most of the components of the mature pattern of these skills. He did not demonstrate any components of the two-handed strike, dribble, hop, or slide. The examiner noted that BT seemed to have adequate strength and flexibility, so physical fitness does not seem to be the reason he does not display these patterns. On the other hand, the examiner suggested that BT may not have been carefully taught the correct components or given time to practice these components. This may explain his delays.

Translating Assessment Results Into a Present Level of Performance

Once results of formal assessments have been interpreted, the next step is to summarize them into a present level of performance (PLOP), or a description of the child's performance in a variety of areas. The PLOP describes the student's strengths and weaknesses and outlines how the disability affects his ability to function in and access the classroom environment. The PLOP is the foundation of the IEP and provides a baseline for developing goals and objectives.

The PLOP should include a summary of the most recent evaluation results, as well as data regarding classroom performance and access to the general curriculum. This PLOP should include both informal and formal assessment data, if appropriate. For example, the sample write-up of a PLOP in appendix 6D includes a summary of results from a standardized assessment, the TGMD-2, as well as observations of Jamal's behaviors and ability to follow directions in PE. However, for students who already have IEP goals, a PLOP might consist of data from alternative assessments of those

goals, general curriculum skills, and observational data from authentic assessments. In appendix 6E, for example, the PLOP discusses information regarding William's ability to participate in the general physical education setting with support, summarizes his progress on meeting current IEP goals of using weight room equipment and riding a bicycle, and includes an assessment of a targeted skill that is difficult for him. Because the PLOP summarizes William's strengths and weaknesses, it helps the IEP team determine what skills he has already mastered and what areas are in need of intervention.

Writing IEP Goals and Objectives Based on the PLOP

After the student's main needs have been narrowed down and prioritized in the PLOP, the next step is to write goals and objectives to address those needs. Long-term goals and short-term objective benchmarks can then be determined based on these recommendations. Long-term IEP goals define the skills the student will learn or master in the next year, whereas the related short-term objectives break down the overall goal into smaller increments.

IEP goals and objectives must be both observable and measurable. Goals must describe the action or skill the student will perform in observable terms (e.g., demonstrate, perform, identify) and include measurable criteria for success (e.g., for 15 minutes continuously, three out of five times, for half a mile). Goals and objectives must also include a description of how the student's progress toward meeting the goal will be evaluated. For example, an objective might read: *John will demonstrate stepping with his opposite foot when performing the underhand roll 9 out of 10 times, based on teacher observation.*

IEP must be functional, or directly applicable to real-world tasks and situations. For example, imagine a child who struggled with an item on the Bruininks-Oseretsky Test of Motor Proficiency (Bruininks & Bruininks, 2005) that required jumping in the air and clapping as many times as possible before landing. Because this task would not be a useful skill for the student in the real world, it would be unreasonable to write an IEP goal focusing on the mastery of this task. Instead, it might be determined that the underlying issue is a lack of leg strength. As a result, a functional IEP goal could be to improve the student's leg strength by increasing the length of time she can pedal a stationary bicycle. This would help her learn a functional skill that she can translate to physical activity in the real world while addressing the needed area for intervention.

Goals and objectives vary greatly from one student to another, because they are individualized to meet each student's unique needs. However, all goals share common characteristics of aligning with identified areas of weakness in the PLOP, being observable and measureable, and focusing on the learning of functional skills. A goal bank with examples of observable and measurable goals that might be appropriate for students with ASD can be found in appendix 6F.

Reporting Assessment Results on Children Who Are Untestable

In rare cases a child with ASD may be so withdrawn or noncompliant that it is virtually impossible to complete an assessment. For some reason the child chooses not to attempt most or all of the assessment items, even with the support of the special education teacher, and even when using the child's reinforcement schedule or structured teaching techniques. Some children simply sit and watch; others stand up when asked but will not try any of the activities. Still others run around the gymnasium or engage in self-stimulatory or aggressive behaviors. Regardless of the reasons, such behaviors make it impossible to determine the child's present level of motor performance and accurately determine whether the child has a significant motor delay. In such cases it is still important to report on the assessment session (see appendix 6G for an example). In most cases it is appropriate to qualify the untestable child for adapted physical education services even if the examiner suspects that the child may not have significant motor delays. The child will most likely not participate in general physical education, even with support, and will require specialized programming. In addition, the child will need intensive instruction on how to learn (follow directions, imitate, and interact appropriately) as well as how to master important motor skills.

Conclusion

Assessment is the key to understanding a child's strengths and needs, and it is essential for deter-mining an appropriate physical education program for a child with ASD. Various assessment tools can be used to gather formal and informal data on a child's motor abilities, including developmental motor assessments such as the Peabody Developmental Motor Scales (Folio & Fewell, 2000); fundamental motor skill assessments such as the Test of Gross Motor Development-2 (Ulrich, 2000); motor ability assessments including the Bruininks-Oseretsky Test of Motor Proficiency (Bruininks & Bruininks, 2005) and the Movement ABC-2 Test (Henderson & Sugden, 2007); physical fitness tests such as the Fitnessgram (2010); sport and lifetime leisure tests such as those developed by Special Olympics (Special Olympics, 2011); and alternate assessments such as rubrics and checklists. A variety of factors should be taken into consideration when selecting an assessment instrument for a child with ASD, including the age of the child, the purpose of the assessment, and the child's ability to understand the test directions (Horvat et al., 2007).

When preparing to conduct an assessment with a child with ASD, teachers can use specific strategies to help the child perform well. Prior to assessing, the teacher should gather background information on the child including medical information, behaviors, and communication skills. The teacher can prepare the child for the upcoming assessment by using strategies such as social stories and schedules and practicing the assessment items. During the assessment, the teacher should incorporate reinforcement programs and teaching styles that are familiar to the child. The arrangement of the environment, visual schedules, visual cues, and breaks may also be helpful during the assessment to help students understand directions and reduce their anxiety. For some children with ASD, authentic assessments that take place in their typical settings may provide more accurate information about their abilities.

Once the formal or informal assessment is completed, the results should be summarized in a PLOP. This information allows the teacher or IEP team (or both) to determine the cause of the student's difficulties and determine whether there is a need for APE services. If APE services are warranted, the assessment results will be central in helping to create appropriate programming, set measurable and observable IEP goals, and determine the appropriate placement for the child in the physical education program.

University of Virginia Initial Observation and Referral Form

Child's name: _____ Evaluator: _____

School: _____ Date: _____

Use this form when first observing a child with a disability who has been referred for adapted physical education. Rate each item based on how the child compares to other children in his or her physical education class.

Physical fitness	Adequate	Needs improvement	Significantly inadequate	Not observed
Performs activities that require upper-body strength (e.g., push-ups, throwing, chest pass)				
Performs activities that require lower-body strength (e.g., running, hopping, kicking)				
Performs activities that require flexibility (e.g., stretching, bending, tumbling)				
Performs activities that require endurance (e.g., mile run, games that involve endurance)				
Body composition (e.g., child's weight and general appearance)				

Gross motor skills	Adequate	Needs improvement	Significantly inadequate	Not observed
Performs nonlocomotor skills (e.g., twisting, turning, balance, bending)				
Moves safely around environment (e.g., dodging, space awareness; directions)				
Uses physical education equipment (e.g., balls, bats, scooters)				
Performs locomotor skills (e.g., running, jumping, galloping, hopping, skipping)				
Performs manipulative skills (e.g., throwing, catching, kicking, striking)				
Dance skills (e.g., rhythm, patterns, creative)				
Plays low-organized games (e.g., relays, tag, teacher-made games)				
Sport skills (e.g., throwing in softball, kicking in soccer, volleyball serve, hitting a tennis ball)				
Plays organized sports (e.g., basketball, soccer)				

Behavior, Cognitive Abilities, and Social Skills in Physical Education

Transition to and from physical education	Adequate	Needs improvement	Significantly inadequate	Not observed
Enters without interruption				
Sits in assigned area				
Stops playing with equipment when asked				
Lines up to leave when asked				

Responding to teacher	Adequate	Needs improvement	Significantly inadequate	Not observed
Remains quiet when teacher is talking				
Follows directions in a timely manner—warm-up				
Follows directions in a timely manner—skill focus				
Follows directions in a timely manner—game				
Accepts feedback from teacher				
Uses positive or appropriate language				

Relating to peers and equipment	Adequate	Needs improvement	Significantly inadequate	Not observed
Works cooperatively with a partner when asked (e.g., shares, takes turns)				
Works cooperatively as a member of a group when asked				
Uses positive or appropriate comments to peers				
Seeks social interactions with peers				
Displays good sporting behavior by avoiding conflict with others				
Uses equipment appropriately				

(continued)

From M. Grenier (ed.), 2014, *Physical education for students with autism spectrum disorders: A comprehensive approach* (Champaign, IL: Human Kinetics).

Effort and self-acceptance	Adequate	Needs improvement	Significantly inadequate	Not observed
Quickly begins the activity once instructed				
Continues to participate independently throughout the activity				
Adapts to new tasks and changes				
Strives to succeed and is motivated to learn				
Accepts his or her own skill whether successful or improving				

Cognitive abilities	Adequate	Needs improvement	Significantly inadequate	Not observed
Understands nonverbal directions				
Understands verbal directions				
Processes multiple-step cues				
Attends to instructions				

From M. Grenier (ed.), 2014, *Physical education for students with autism spectrum disorders: A comprehensive approach* (Champaign, IL: Human Kinetics).

Sample Rubrics for Alternate Assessments

Major league	Independently walks into gym and finds spot or squad to sit down and wait for instructions.
AAA	With verbal or picture prompt just in front of gym door, walks into gym and finds spot or squad to sit down and wait for instructions.
AA	With verbal or picture prompt in front of gym door and second prompt once in gym, walks into gym and finds spot or squad to sit down and wait for instructions.
A	Needs multiple verbal or picture prompts before entering gym and then to find spot or squad and sit down to wait for instructions.
Rookie league	Needs multiple verbal or picture prompts as well as gesture prompts before entering gym and then to find spot or squad and sit down to wait for instructions.

Rubric for Walking Into the Gym and Finding a Spot

Rating	Description
Major league	Independently walks into gym and finds spot or squad to sit down and wait for instructions.
AAA	With verbal or picture prompt just in front of gym door, walks into gym and finds spot or squad to sit down and wait for instructions.
AA	With verbal or picture prompt in front of gym door and second prompt once in gym, walks into gym, finds spot or squad, and sits down waiting for instructions.
A	Needs multiple verbal or picture prompts before entering gym and then to find spot or squad and sit down to wait for instructions.
Rookie league	Needs multiple verbal or picture prompts as well as gesture prompts before entering gym and then to find spot or squad and sit down to wait for instructions.

Rubric for Following Multiple-Step Directions

Rating	Description
Team Alpha	Follows directions with three or more steps independently.
Team Beta	Follows directions with three or more steps with one verbal or picture prompt.
Team Gamma	Follows directions with three or more steps with two or three verbal or picture prompts.
Team Delta	Follows directions with three or more steps with multiple verbal or picture prompts.
Team Epsilon	Needs multiple verbal or picture prompts as well as gesture prompts to follow directions with three or more steps.

(continued)

Rubric for Sitting and Waiting

Rating	Description
MVP	Independently sits and listens to directions for up to four minutes.
All-Star 1	With one verbal or picture prompt will sit and listen to directions for up to four minutes.
All-Star 2	With two or three verbal or picture prompts will sit and listen to directions for up to four minutes.
All-Star 3	Needs multiple verbal or picture prompts to sit and listen to directions for up to four minutes.
All-Star 4	Needs multiple verbal or picture prompts and gestures or physical prompts to sit and listen to directions for up to four minutes.

Rubric for the Overhand Throw

Rating	Description
Orioles	With verbal or picture cue, throws using all of the components of a skillful throw.
Nationals	With verbal or picture cue, throws using five out of six components of the skillful throw.
Yankees	With verbal or picture cue, throws using four out of six components of the skillful throw.
Red Sox	With verbal or picture cue, throws using three out of six components of the skillful throw.
Rockies	With verbal or picture cue, throws using two out of six components of the skillful throw.
Angels	With verbal or picture cue, tosses ball forward.
Dodgers	With verbal or picture cue, puts ball into bucket.

Components of a Skillful Throw

1. Orients sideways to target.
2. Shifts weight to back foot and makes a T with arms.
3. Bends throwing elbow so ball is near ear.
4. Shifts weight forward and steps with opposite foot.
5. Releases ball just past head.
6. Follows through so hand approaches opposite knee.

From M. Grenier (ed.), 2014, *Physical education for students with autism spectrum disorders: A comprehensive approach* (Champaign, IL: Human Kinetics).

Sample Assessment Report
Based on the Test of Gross Motor Development

Adapted Physical Education Observation and Evaluation

Name: BT

DOB: February 4, 2005

Date: October 27, 2013

School: Any

Evaluator: Martin Block, PhD, CAPE

Background Information

BT is an eight-year-old male student with ASD who attends Any School. BT does not currently receive physical education, and his parents requested an evaluation to determine whether he qualifies for adapted physical education services. BT was tested using the Test of Gross Motor Development-2 (TGMD-2). He was tested in the gross motor room at Any School by Dr. Martin Block of the kinesiology program at the University of Virginia. BT was supported during testing by his teacher. There were two other students in the gross motor room during testing, but BT did not seem distracted by them. BT was cooperative during all testing, first watching a demonstration of the targeted skill (e.g., throwing) and then attempting to perform the skill three to five times. When necessary, a second demonstration or physical assistance was provided to make sure he knew what he was supposed to do. I believe these test results are a fair representation of BT's current gross motor skills.

Test of Gross Motor Development-2

The TGMD-2 is an individually administered norm- and criterion-referenced test that measures the gross motor functioning of children 3 to 10 years of age. The test measures 12 gross motor skills frequently taught to children in preschool and elementary school. The skills are grouped into two subtests: locomotion and object control. The locomotion subtest measures the run, gallop, hop, leap, horizontal jump, skip, and slide. The object control subtest measures the two-hand strike, stationary dribble, catch, kick, overhand throw, and underhand roll. Each of these motor skills has been broken down into three to five components. Components are analyzed to determine whether the component was present (1) or not present (0). Results were then tallied across two trials and totaled for locomotor and object control subtests. Finally, each subtest score was compared to a normative sample for analysis. The following report presents BT's results on the TGMD-2.

BT scored in the first percentile for the locomotor and object control skills (age equivalent of <2.5 years) compared to eight-year-olds in the norm sample. BT performed best on the run, in which he demonstrated all of the components of a mature run during one trial. However, he was inconsistent in his run; on many of the trials he performed a fast walk rather than a run. He also was able to take off and land on two feet for the jump, although he did not use his arms to help in the jump. He could hop on one foot once or twice, and he demonstrated the basic gallop and slide in one out of four trials but only after much prompting. In object control skills, BT was able to demonstrate the basic form of the kick, overhand throw, and catch. However, he did not demonstrate any of the components of a mature pattern. For example, with throwing he did not rotate his body to the side or step with the opposite foot; with the catch he did not reach to meet the ball or use his hands to catch; and with the kick he did not step next to the ball, bend his leg in preparation for the kick, or follow through. It should be noted that BT may not have been exposed to or practiced the correct patterns of these object control skills, which may explain why he did not demonstrate

(continued)

many of these components. BT appears to have normal strength, flexibility, endurance, balance, and coordination, and with practice and instruction there is no reason to believe BT cannot learn how to perform these locomotor and object control skills at a more skillful level.

Summary and Recommendations

BT's performance on the Test of Gross Motor Development-2 shows he has significant delays in gross motor development. As noted earlier, these delays are probably due in large part to lack of exposure to and instruction in these specific patterns rather than any physical or motor deficit. Regardless, he is functioning at a significant delay in gross motor development, and as a result he does qualify for adapted physical education (APE) services. Given his delays, I am recommending APE services for a total of 60 minutes (two times per week for 30 minutes per session) starting immediately in a one-on-one setting. I recommend goals that focus on basic locomotor and object control skills. Specifically, I recommend two locomotor objectives (jump and slide) and two object control skills (catch and kick). I also recommend asking his parents for input about the specific gross motor skills they would like to see BT master during APE.

Martin Block

_____

Martin Block, PhD, CAPE
Kinesiology Program
Curry School of Education
University of Virginia

Sample Present Level of Performance and Corresponding IEP Goals From TGMD-2 Results

Sample Present Level of Performance Including Formal Assessment Data

Jamal is a seven-year-old child who has been diagnosed as having ASD. He attends Mrs. Block's class for children with ASD. Jamal is generally physically fit with average to above-average flexibility, upper- and lower-body strength (can climb and jump very well), endurance (can run on the playground for several minutes without stopping or getting winded), and body composition. Jamal has mastered all basic loco-motor skills (run, jump, hop, skip), but he does not do these movements on command. He has the basic patterns for object control skills such as kicking, throwing, striking, and catching, but he does not use the correct components when performing these skills. Finally, Jamal has a difficult time quietly entering the gymnasium with his nondisabled classmates and finding his spot to sit. He will sit for only one or two minutes and listen to directions before he gets up and runs around the room, and he has difficulty following multiple-step directions.

Sample IEP Goals

- The student will independently enter gymnasium, find designated squad, and sit down in squad with one verbal prompt three out of four days.
- The student will independently follow a three-step direction during physical education class three out of four days.
- With one or two verbal or picture reminders, the student will sit quietly and listen to instructions given by the general physical education teacher for up to four minutes three out of four days.
- With one verbal or picture cue, the student will demonstrate three out of six components of the overhand throw so that the ball travels 7 to 10 feet (2 to 3 m) in the air toward a target three out of four days.

Present Level of Performance on Existing IEP Goals and Authentic Assessment Results

William is a student who has ASD and currently receives adapted physical education (APE) in both a small-group and one-on-one setting. During the first semester, William received APE in the general physical education setting as well.

William participated in a ninth-grade general physical education (GPE) class during the first semester and responded well to the class environment. William attended GPE with the help of a teacher assistant and a special education teacher who provided assistance as needed. William required some verbal cues to remain on task during activities and follow directions. He did have difficulty transitioning between activities during PE, but needed less verbal prompting as he became familiar with the routine. William had the opportunity to become familiar with modified organized sports including basketball, volleyball, and soccer. Although William did well during skill development activities, he had difficulty keeping up with the pace of group games.

William has been introduced to all of the equipment in the weight room, including the leg press, lat pull-down, hand weight exercises, leg extension, and leg curl. He is able to follow a color-coded word schedule in the weight room to independently move to each piece of equipment. He has improved in his ability to tolerate noise and activity levels in the weight room, but continues to have difficulty with large groups. William needs assistance to set the weight on each machine and needs verbal cues, modeling, and some physical assistance to use the proper technique.

William also has been introduced to riding an adapted adult tricycle. William is able to pedal the bicycle independently, but needs assistance to fasten his helmet, steer, and brake. William is able to pedal a stationary and adapted bicycle for two minutes at a moderate pace before tiring.

William has also been evaluated on his ability to perform skills related to baseball. Although William is able to perform many of these activities, he does not perform the correct components of each skill. For example, William is able to throw a ball to a partner, but does not step in opposition, turn his side to the target, or follow through when throwing. He is unable to catch fly balls. William does attempt to field ground balls rolled directly to him, but has difficulty bending at the waist and does not squeeze the ball in his glove.

It is recommended that William continue to receive 60 minutes of APE per week to improve his muscular strength, object control skills, and lifetime leisure skills. Instruction may take place in the GPE setting, in a small-group setting, or one on one as needed. William would benefit from increased participation in community-based physical activities such as bowling and hiking.

Corresponding IEP Goals

- The student will perform the overhand throw, performing all of the components correctly 8 out of 10 times with verbal cues.
- The student will successfully catch a ball rolled directly to him using a baseball glove by moving the glove to the ball and squeezing the ball in the glove 7 out of 10 times with verbal cues.
- The student will participate in a stretching and exercise routine following a picture schedule and perform two sets of 10 repetitions of each exercise correctly with verbal cues and modeling.
- The student will appropriately participate in two lifetime leisure activities with peers by taking turns and participating as appropriate four out of five times.

Sample IEP Goal Bank

Fitness

- The student will walk 1 mile (1.6 km) continuously, without stopping, two out of five times with a teacher or peer.
- The student will perform 15 consecutive modified curl-ups with decreasing assistance.
- The student will perform one set of 10 repetitions of each designated upper-body strength activity using hand weights, weight room equipment, or a Thera-Band, using correct technique with assistance.
- The student will complete 1 mile (1.6 km) around the track or other facilities in 15 minutes alongside a peer or adult.
- The student will participate in a stretching and exercise routine, following a visual schedule and performing two sets of 10 repetitions of each exercise three out of five times with verbal cues.
- The student will perform two sets of 10 repetitions of designated upper-body strength activities, using the correct technique four out of five times with verbal cues.
- The student will perform regular curl-ups 20 consecutive times with feet stabilized, with verbal prompting.
- The student will use two pieces of weight room equipment 10 consecutive times, using proper technique without physical assistance.
- The student will walk on the treadmill for 10 minutes at a speed of 2.5 miles per hour (4 km/h) independently.
- The student will pedal a stationary bicycle independently for eight minutes continuously.
- The student will perform five consecutive push-ups using proper technique with visual cues.
- The student will perform two sets of 10 repetitions of the arm curl, bench press, and overhead press using 8-pound (3.6 kg) hand weights independently.
- The student will remain physically active for 15-minute intervals during individual or group activities, independently.
- The student will perform simple warm-up stretches three out of five times with assistance.
- The student will jog continuously for 0.5 mile (0.8 km) in seven minutes, in three out of five trials, with verbal cues and modeling.

Lifetime Sport Skills

- The student will perform a basic forehand tennis stroke using proper technique and making contact with the ball independently in a nongame situation.
- The student will perform the forehand tennis stroke using proper technique according to the county curriculum, making contact with the ball two out of five times independently, when hitting a ball served or tossed directly to her.
- The student will perform the golf putt, setting himself correctly before each swing and swinging with appropriate force 7 out of 10 times independently.
- The student will grip the golf club correctly four out of five times with minimal verbal cues.
- The student will perform the back float independently for 10 seconds, four out of five times.
- The student will perform a front crawl stroke a distance of 10 meters independently using correct arm motions.

Team Sport Skills

- The student will shoot a basketball using proper hand placement and using her legs for power 6 out of 10 times with minimal verbal prompting.

(continued)

- The student will shoot a basketball using proper technique 6 out of 10 times independently.
- The student will dribble up to shoot using proper dribbling technique 6 out of 10 times with minimal verbal prompting.
- The student will remain physically active during large-group activities for 10-minute intervals with minimal assistance.

Object Control Skills

- The student will perform the correct components of the underhand roll, according to the county PE curriculum, three out of five times with minimal verbal cues and modeling.
- The student will catch a ball or beanbag tossed directly to him using only his hands three out of five times with minimal physical assistance.
- The student will perform the underhand roll, using one hand and stepping with the foot opposite the preferred hand, one out of five times with modeling and verbal cues.
- The student will participate in gross motor activities such as kicking, rolling, tossing, and catching, with an adult or peer, sustaining activity for three turns, with physical assistance and verbal cues.
- The student will catch a ball tossed directly to her while in a standing position three out of five times with decreasing assistance.
- The student will throw a beanbag to a target from 1 foot (30 cm) away, three out of five times with decreasing assistance.
- The student will perform the stationary basketball dribble, using the finger pads and keeping the ball below waist height, eight times continuously with the preferred hand.

Locomotor Skills

- The student will demonstrate the following components of the gallop on three out of five trials with minimal physical assistance and modeling: arms flexed at sides and lifted to waist level at takeoff; step with lead foot followed by step with rear foot; maintain rhythmical pattern.
- The student will perform the slide, maintaining a sideways body position and direction of travel for three step-slide cycles in each direction with minimal physical assistance.
- The student will perform the hop, taking off and landing on one foot three times continuously, in three out of five trials with minimal physical assistance.

Affective

- The student will follow two-step directions during PE activities three out of five times with minimal verbal cues.
- The student will remain on task during small-group activities for 10-minute intervals four out of five times with minimal verbal cues.
- The student will work cooperatively with a partner for five-minute intervals independently.
- The student will participate in large-group activities, remaining physically active for five-minute intervals with minimal verbal cues.
- The student will take turns and participate as appropriate in lifetime leisure activities with peers in four out of five trials with minimal verbal cues and modeling.
- The student will participate cooperatively with a peer during partner activities, taking turns as appropriate in 8 out of 10 trials with assistance.

Sample Write-Up for a Child Who Is Untestable

Introduction

Harry Smith is a five-year-old male child with ASD. He currently attends a class for children with ASD at Blue Ridge School. Due to behaviors, Harry has not been attending general physical education (GPE) classes, and a request was placed to assess Harry to determine whether he qualified for adapted physical education (APE) services. Mr. Block and Ms. Taliaferro, APE specialists for the district, assessed Harry.

Testing

The Peabody Developmental Motor Scales-2 (PDMS-2) was used to test Harry. The test has three subtests: stationary, locomotion, and object manipulation skills. The stationary subtest measures skills such as standing on one foot, standing on tiptoes, and imitating movements. The locomotion subtest measures such skills as hopping, jumping, and running. The object manipulation subtest measures such skills as bouncing a ball, hitting a target with a ball, and kicking a ball. Testing was administered in the auxiliary gym at Blue Ridge School. Harry and his examiners were the only people present during testing.

Unfortunately, we were unable to test Harry using the PDMS-2. We were unable to get Harry to focus on and understand what to do on the test, even after providing verbal instructions, physical cues, and visual demonstrations. It should be noted that after we stopped formally testing Harry, we did allow him some time to explore the gymnasium. During this time we were able to observe him running and playing with balls. He was very active and seemed to enjoy kicking soccer balls. Nevertheless, we were unable to gather enough information to determine objectively whether Harry was delayed in gross motor development.

Summary and Recommendations

Harry is a five-year-old male with ASD who currently receives special education services through the autism program at Blue Ridge School. We attempted to test Harry, but because of his behaviors, we were unable to get any objective data. Regardless, we believe that Harry does qualify for APE services. Given his behaviors, we recommend that Harry receive 60 minutes of one-on-one APE services per week focusing initially on helping him follow directions and stay on task with gross motor activities.

Andrea Taliaferro and Martin Block, APE Specialists
Blue Ridge School District

PART II

Individual and Small-Group Games and Activities

Individualized Games and Activities

Ann Griffin

"I just got assigned two adapted PE classes of students with autism. I don't know any of the kids. I don't know where to start in my planning. What should I do?" Although this statement is often uttered in panic at a new teaching assignment, physical educators will find that they have many tools in their professional tool kits that are directly applicable to teaching students with autism spectrum disorders (ASD). Physical educators develop warm-up exercises and routines. They get to know student interests. They help students learn to move and play and have fun while moving. They assess motor, fitness, and sport skills. They understand skill development and can plan challenges for a variety of skill levels. All of these skills can be applied to working with students with ASD.

The activity suggestions in this chapter are intended to help educators begin to apply the skills they have to their unique populations of students with ASD. Although designed for use in small-group adapted physical education (APE) classes, these activities, stations, and equipment may be readily used in the general physical education program as well. Activities are organized into four sections:

1. **Class routine and warm-up exercises.** When working with students with ASD, physical educators need to teach class routines explicitly. Activities in this section include suggestions for teaching laps and warm-up exercises.
2. **Station activities using equipment turn-ons.** These station activities address the unique interests of students with ASD by making use of physical education equipment likely to engage activity. Getting to know students' individual interests is critical to student engagement and planning.
3. **Play skill and social interaction activities.** These activities teach play skills and naturally encourage peer interaction through a "cool" factor—that is, equipment that naturally attracts attention. We call such equipment kid magnets because they are fun to use with friends or require friends to operate, and they encourage children to play.
4. **Motor and sport skill stations.** These practice stations are arranged according to skill or sport units. Prior to participation in small-sided or lead-up games, students with ASD need opportunities to practice the game-related skills with a variety of equipment.

Class Routine and Warm-Up Exercises

Because students with ASD like routines, establishing a clear class routine should be one of the first steps in planning. The routine helps minimize stress and provides an active transition. Many classes begin with laps or "move around the gym" instant activities, followed by some sort of warm-up routine. Modeling APE warm-up routines after those used in general physical education (GPE) is a good way to prepare students with ASD for later participation in GPE warm-ups. Before having students perform the routine, physical educators should teach and model it (e.g., laps, exercises on the mats, station or small-group activities, clean-up). The routine can be written on a whiteboard or provided to students in individual schedules if needed.

This section offers lap, exercise, and warm-up suggestions. Four Corners, Four Cones teaches students to run laps and gets them moving upon entering the gym. Exercise decks, cubes, and dice can be used to vary the visual representation of warm-up exercises. A fitness ball routine is an invitation to warm up and move. Ask cards provide visual instructions for balance and body awareness warm-ups.

Four Corners, Four Cones: Move Around the Cones

Four Corners, Four Cones is a way to vary laps and provide practice, modeling, and instruction for a variety of locomotor movements and sport skills. This activity teaches students to move around the perimeter of the gym, which is a typical arrangement for running laps in physical education classes. This flexible approach to moving around the gym can easily be generalized to other gyms, unmarked recreation areas, and outdoor activity spaces.

Motor Skill Objectives   Instant movement, warm-up, locomotor skills, functional assessment of fitness; helps to establish a predictable routine.

Age Range   Preschool, primary (K-2), intermediate (3-5), middle school (6-8), high school (9-12), 18+; readily adaptable to any age group.

Social Skill Objectives   Turn taking, starting and stopping activities, working in groups.

Equipment and Materials Needed   Initially, just four cones; then add cone task cards to direct the skill focus (figure 7.1).

PROCEDURE

Place four cones in the center of the gym. The objective is to teach students to move around the gym for warm-up laps. Some students naturally run on the line or trail the wall; others move randomly. Begin with the cones in the center of the gym and model running, walking, galloping, marching, and moving to music around the cones. Move with the students, modeling a variety of locomotor movements. Increase the distance between the cones over time. Once the cones are close to the four corners of the gym, add task cards to direct locomotor movements. Students can check the task card at the sideline or end line for how to move around the cones.

FIGURE 7.1 This task card provides a visual cue telling students how to move around the cones.

HELPFUL HINTS AND MODIFICATIONS

- Use music and watch the students to get a feel for the volume level that works best.
- Initially just have students "move around the cones or gym" and model a variety of movements.
- Start with one task card that gives a choice of the activity (e.g., walk or jog); add a second card (to indicate a change in movement), then a third, and eventually a fourth.
- Vary the locomotor skills and task cards to include run, skip, gallop, walk, march, basketball slide, animal walks, and so on (see figure 7.2).
- Cone task cards, such as the one in figure 7.2, can be easily made out of manila file folders. Simply glue a number, Boardmaker icon, photo, or catalog picture to the file folder, laminate the folder, and cut a hole in the center. The task card slips easily over any cone.
- Have students use quick movements on the long sides of the gym, such as jog, skip, gallop, slide-step, and run.
- Have them use slow movements on the short side of the gym, such as crab walk, hop, jump, seal walk, logroll, bear walk, and knee walk.
- Provide a row of mats on one end line of the gym for low-level locomotor movements such as log-rolls and animal walks.
- Provide a way for students to keep track of the number of laps (e.g., clothespins, deck tennis rings placed on cones, popsicle sticks, basketball stickers).
- Use pedometers to see exactly how much activity you are getting out of the students.
- Add a lap enticement such as a big slide (e.g., "First, run around the gym; then slide again"). This channels random activity into an instructional pattern with lots of applications. The slide is the reinforcer (see figure 7.3).
- Add other activities while you are moving around the gym with the students. Pair up with a student and get his attention while moving. Cue him with "Ready? Set, go" and race down an end line or sideline. Add a balance beam on an end line. Dribble a basketball a length or lap, or dribble a soccer ball. This activity lends itself to many uses across classes.

FIGURE 7.2 Task cards and cone markers indicating student movement: march, airplane walk (arms extended like airplane wings), or jog.

FIGURE 7.3 Placing a slide on one of the corners of the gym will entice students to run another lap. "Run around, slide . . . do it again!"

Exercise Deck

Exercise Deck is a visual warm-up activity in which students draw playing cards that indicate warm-up exercises. The number, or value, of the playing card tells the student how many repetitions of the exercise to do.

Motor Skill Objectives Addresses multiple areas of fitness including strength and flexibility.

Age Range Preschool, primary (K-2), intermediate (3-5), middle school (6-8), high school (9-12), 18+.

Social Skill Objectives Turn taking if played with a partner, working independently.

Equipment and Materials Needed Poly spots (as many as you have cards) and decks of exercise playing cards. The exercise decks can be made with new or used decks of playing cards, exercise symbols from Boardmaker, and clear packing tape. The exercise icons from the program are printed in 1¼-inch (3.2 cm) format, cut apart, and taped onto the face of the playing cards with the clear packing tape (see figure 7.4).

FIGURE 7.4 Exercise icons are taped to the playing cards and include toe touches, jumping jacks, arm circles, leg lifts, push-ups, and sit-ups. Each student draws a card and does the indicated exercise that number of times.

PROCEDURE

Scatter poly spots around the playing area. Place an exercise playing card facedown on each spot. This prevents students from preselecting an exercise or *not* selecting a certain exercise. Ask students to move about the play area, select a spot, turn over the card, and do the exercise the designated number of times on the playing card. They then place the card facedown when finished. Students move to a certain number of spots, such as five. You can give them a choice (e.g., five or six) or say, "How many can you get to before the music stops?"

HELPFUL HINTS AND MODIFICATIONS

- Teach each exercise from the deck prior to having the students play the game.
- If face cards are problematic, (i.e., jack, queen, and king = 10), begin with only numerical cards.
- Provide a separate cue card that clearly indicates how much an ace or face card is worth (e.g., ace = 11, king = 10, queen = 10, jack = 10, and so on).
- Provide a peer partner to model the exercises and count.
- Exercise cubes and dice provide an alternative to a deck of cards. Students toss the exercise cube and a die or dice to receive an exercise and the number of repetitions (see figure 7.5).
- Use commercially available Fit-Deck exercise cards in a similar format.
- Use exercise Hot Spots, which are exercise- and equipment-specific poly spots that provide both visual and written cues. A variety of sets are available including ones for core exercises, exercise tubing, medicine balls, fitness balls, partner exercises, yoga, and jump roping.

FIGURE 7.5 Students roll the exercise cube and the die or dice and do the exercise the indicated number of times.

- Make a photo warm-up book so students can see photos of people performing the warm-up exercises.

Fitness Ball Warm-Up

Necessity is the mother of invention. In one of our APE classes, the enthusiasm for the warm-up routine was gone. Students refused to follow any exercise warm-up routine we modeled. They didn't want to move! They simply sat down. It was obvious that an instructional change was needed. We broke out our secret weapons: the big red fitness balls! When the students entered the gym, they saw the balls and sat on them . . . and then they began to move and bounce, and *exercise*.

Motor Skill Objectives   Addresses various areas of fitness including strength and flexibility and engagement with equipment.

Age Range   Intermediate (3-5), middle school (6-8), high school (9-12), 18+.

Social Skill Objectives   Small-group activity participation.

Equipment and Materials Needed   Fitness balls (one per person). Provide a variety of sizes. The general rule for choosing the correct fitness ball size for exercises is that the knees and hips should be bent to 90 degrees (thighs parallel to floor) when sitting on the ball. Provide balls for peer assistants as well so they can be eye-level models for students.

PROCEDURE

Place hula hoops on the floor in a semicircle. Place a fitness ball in each hula hoop. This formation increases the chances that students follow teacher or peer models (see figure 7.6). Seated on a fitness ball in the center of the semicircle, model a variety of exercises and activities. If students do not follow your lead, try imitating their actions to engage them. Exercise possibilities include strength activities such as sit-ups and push-ups on the ball, upper-body warm-ups (seated bounce with arm movements), and bouncing for fitness.

HELPFUL HINTS AND MODIFICATIONS

- As with all pieces of high-interest or new equipment, provide a period of freestyle, or free, play before attempting to lead a lesson. This gives you an opportunity to assess student interest and skill and note any potential safety issues.

- Use the DVD that came with the equipment if available.

- Create a DVD of the students performing their exercise routines.

- Use music to help pace the activity.

FIGURE 7.6   Hula hoops provide the structure and semicircle formation for the Fitness Ball Warm-Up activity. The teacher leads the activity from the center.

Can You Do It? I Can Do It!

Eric Carle's book *From Head to Toe* illustrates a great full-body warm-up routine that reinforces body awareness. With students standing in a circle on poly spots, read the book, showing the students the pictures and modeling each movement. For example, say, "I am a penguin and I can turn my head. Can you do it?" Students respond, "I can do it" and model the movement or exercise. The book proceeds through body parts from head to toe, providing an all-over stretch and warm-up. Once students have learned the movements in the book, they are ready to use the Head to Toe card game.

Motor Skill Objectives   Active engagement, body part identification.

Age Range   Preschool, primary (K-2).

Social Skill Objectives   Small-group participation, modeling.

Equipment and Materials Needed   Eric Carle's card game From Head to Toe and one round, plastic tablecloth (dollar stores are good sources for tablecloths).

PROCEDURE

The tablecloth provides the designated area for game play. Draw 12 rectangles to indicate card placement. From Head to Toe cards are placed facedown on each rectangle (see figure 7.7). Each tablecloth is a station at which two or three students can comfortably work. They may work individually on their own cards or play together. Students move to a card, turn it over so that it is "action side up," and do the exercise. When finished, they replace the card and move to another. Determine the number of exercises you would like students to do. The tablecloth provides a great visual structure for the game, making setup easy. Fuzzy-backed tablecloths stick nicely to carpet for classroom use.

HELPFUL HINTS AND MODIFICATIONS

- Use poly spots around the perimeter of the tablecloth so students know where to stand or move. Spots numbered 1 through 12 can indicate the direction of movement.

- Have students stand in a circle formation (on poly spots) and do the activity while you read the book.

FIGURE 7.7   A round, plastic tablecloth provides organizational structure for the From Head to Toe card game. Action cards are placed facedown. Students flip the card to reveal movement challenge: "I am a giraffe and I can move my neck . . . Can you do it?" The cards in the foreground are "action side up."

Monkey See, Monkey Do

Students imitate the pose that is depicted on the task card, individually or with a partner. Monkey See, Monkey Do is a warm-up activity that gives students an opportunity to stretch and balance in a variety of planes while working alone or with a partner.

Motor Skill Objectives   Body awareness, balance.

Age Range   Preschool, primary (K-2), intermediate (3-5).

Social Skill Objectives   Imitation, cooperation with a partner.

Equipment and Materials Needed   One small activity mat per student and one set of Monkey See, Monkey Do posters. Glue the directions to the back of the card. The directions include three symbols: a bow or tie to indicate the body part, a body indicating the position (standing, sitting, lying down), and a head indicating verbal directions that you might give from the front of the class.

PROCEDURE

Exercise mats are scattered throughout the play area, one student per mat. Place three or four cards on each exercise mat. Show the student the pose and say, "Do this" (figure 7.8). Model or assist as necessary.

HELPFUL HINTS AND MODIFICATIONS

- Begin by having students simply imitate the poses. Don't have them both assume the pose *and* place the tie or sweatband on the appropriate body part during the initial stages of game play.

- Individual poses are easier than poses involving a classmate or peer. Move from simple to complex.

- Initially, an adult may need to be the partner.

- Because students with ASD are three-dimensional thinkers, they may demonstrate poses in unexpected planes. The directions may indicate "standing," but the student may lie flat on her back. Without verbal directions, this would also be a correct response to the pose.

- Ties on the limbs of the monkey can be used for practicing left and right. Sweatbands work well as ties because they are easily slid on and off arms and legs. Students move the sweatbands from right arm to left ankle, as indicated by the monkey.

FIGURE 7.8   Imitating a pose from a Monkey See, Monkey Do card.

Station Activities Using Equipment Turn-Ons

Children with ASD often have trouble learning how to play and work with others. Many have difficulty engaging in directed physical education activities. Some wander through a gym full of equipment and never seem to notice anything. Others explode into the gym and tear through the space with mad abandon. Teachers need to entice them to participate or focus their enthusiasm. Knowing what students like and do not like is very helpful in getting them to play and learn motor skills. For example, children who are interested in wheels can have lots of fun with bikes, scooters, and wagons. Those who like to climb do well on climbing walls and obstacle courses.

Many students are interested in particular features of objects or equipment rather than their function. There could be a fascination with "black holes" such as electrical outlets, nostrils, tubes, and heating grates. Rather than labeling students' fascinations as weird or inappropriate, teachers can try using that fascination to get their attention and engage them in physical education. If a student seems interested in holes, the physical educator can look for items with holes such as Wiffle balls, bowling balls, and deck tennis rings.

If a student is interested in black holes, the teacher can try using a few of the items depicted in figure 7.9. By using interesting, novel equipment that purposefully incorporates individual interests, teachers can begin to shape students' motor and play behaviors, broaden their interests, and increase their skill repertoire.

FIGURE 7.9 Look at your equipment through the eyes of the student. If a student likes to play with the batons, try broadening his interest with other items that have holes.

Equipment Turn-Ons: Stations for Engagement

The stations in this section will help physical educators get to know their students' interests. Because many students with ASD are difficult to engage in play or physical education activities, these stations are set up using high-interest equipment, or turn-ons. This list of turn-ons has evolved over time based on the unique, individual, and sensory interests of students with ASD, such as holes and strings or small spaces, pressure, spinning, or jumping. By providing equipment likely to get their attention and engage them in activity, physical educators have the opportunity to assess their interests and skills. Appendix 7A at the end of this chapter provides a comprehensive list of turn-ons.

Motor Skill Objectives Interaction with physical education equipment, student interest assessment.

Age Range Preschool, primary (K-2), intermediate (3-5), middle school (6-8), high school (9-12), 18+.

Social Skill Objectives Equipment interaction, peer interaction, turn taking, starting and stopping activities, changing activities.

Equipment and Materials Needed Six cones numbered 1 through 6. Select equipment for each station based on the list of equipment turn-ons in appendix 7A or known student interest. The pieces of equipment on the list are student approved.

PROCEDURE

Set up six stations around the gym and identify them with cones. Select equipment from the turn-on list for each station: ball play, balance, wheels, rocking and spinning, pressure, and jumping and bouncing. Initially, provide *no* instruction. Rather, simply observe, videotape, note, and record students' interests. Use an informal assessment tool to track student interests and interactions with equipment or other items in the space (e.g., curtains, doors, light switches). Appendixes 7B and 7C provide recording forms for informally assessing students at stations. After a period of observation, try to engage with the student. Mirror his equipment choices and actions; then do something different with the same piece of equipment. Try to engage play. Play next to the student to see if he will model your actions. Make an attempt to engage students at each of the stations.

HELPFUL HINTS AND MODIFICATIONS

- A station framework may be used for all ages. Please make an effort to keep equipment age appropriate (i.e., equipment that same-age peers would be interested in using).
- Maintain the stations and vary the equipment at each one.
- Stations can be adapted to provide a unit related to a particular skill such as jumping or balance.
- Use stations to preassess students at the beginning of the school year or any new unit.

Ball Station: Equipment Choices

Finding the right type, size, color, weight, shape, and texture of ball is the key to engaging students in beginning ball play and manipulative skills. Use the informal assessment form in appendix 7B or 7C to note individual student interest. During the observation, or free play, portion of the lesson, carefully observe what students do at this station. Note which balls they interact with and what they do with them (e.g., bounce, roll, throw overhead backward, smell, bang into chin, drum, kick). Which balls do they touch, and which do they avoid? During the engagement portion of the lesson, model a variety of ball skills such as rolling, throwing overhand and underhand, throwing to a target, tossing to self, bouncing and catching, and dribbling with the hands or feet. Following are some balls you might use:

- Slo-Mo Bump balls are easy to catch, bounce, and grab with one hand and are fairly lightweight (*not* good for biters) (see figure 7.10).
- Koosh balls drop and don't roll away when tossing and catching; they are good for kids who like strings.
- Sensation balls provide both visual and auditory feedback. They can be variably inflated for grip or bounce.
- Inside-out balls are fairly heavy and can go on your hand, on another ball, or on your head! They don't roll away if you miss when playing catch.
- Grab balls with tails are easy to swing or catch by the tail and visually interesting; holes in the

FIGURE 7.10 Student sorts sensation balls, grab balls with tails, Kixz balls (foam balls with holes), and Slo-Mo Bump balls.

balls make them easy to catch (see Ribbon Ball Station Card in appendix 7D). Additionally, the ribbons can be detached so students use just the ball or just the ribbon. Objects made of Mylar or other materials may be inserted into the ball for another sensory experience.

- Spider balls slow down when rolled, so they don't get too far away. These are also fun for kids who like strings (see figure 7.11).

- Suction balls are fun for rolling on the floor with the flat of the hand and make an interesting noise. They can be thrown at whiteboards or windows for tic-tac-toe or target games.

FIGURE 7.11   Spider balls (have strings that function as brakes) are used to roll and knock down bowling pins.

HELPFUL HINTS AND MODIFICATIONS

- Have a huge variety of multisensory balls.
- Pet stores are excellent sources of affordable, durable, washable, and multisensory balls.
- Make the station visually stimulating by including streamers, holes, color, movement, and lights.
- Use a variety of balls (e.g., soft, hard, large, small, light, heavy).
- Use a variety of noise-making balls.
- Have a good supply of each kind of equipment for sharing.
- Keep doing the same things; students with ASD require multiple turns and repeated trials to begin to learn motor skills.
- Provide buckets, racks, baskets, or ball carts for storing equipment during class.
- Larger balls such as soccer balls and basketballs sit nicely on deck tennis rings, marking where they should be replaced.

Balance Station: Equipment Choices

Many students with ASD love balance challenges. Balance beams of varying heights, stilts, floor ladders, incline beams, wedges, and stacks of mats can provide a wide range of balance activities in the gym. During the observation, or free play, section of the lesson, watch to see what students attempt at this station. Later, engage with them by playing follow the leader or providing support for untried balance activities.

- You can construct balance courses with what you have on hand. Popular components include stability pads (figure 7.12), step boxes, and river rock stepping stones (figure 7.13).

FIGURE 7.12   Stability pads provide students with an opportunity to practice balance activities in standing or sitting positions.

- Bubble wrap can be used to make a wide balance path and provide a little tactile and auditory feedback, too. Tactile paths can be made out of bathtub footprints and bathmats cut into strips. These have the added benefit of sticking to the gym floor with suction cups (see figure 7.14).
- Slack lines are great for outdoor balance work. They also tend to draw lots of friends!

FIGURE 7.13 River rocks provide a flexible balance challenge.

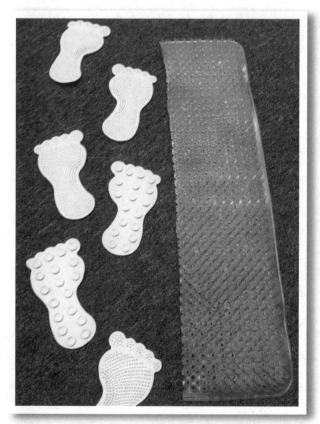

FIGURE 7.14 Bathtub footprints can be used as a tactile path.

HELPFUL HINTS AND MODIFICATIONS

Provide a variety of balance challenges and equipment. Students with ASD tend to excel at balance activities, although some may dislike having their feet off the ground or on different surfaces. The playground provides lots of opportunities for students to experience movement on a variety of surfaces. They can move from blacktop to shredded tires to pea gravel to grass. Just walking over a variety of surfaces helps build students' confidence. Ice and snow offer very interesting winter balance challenges. Indoors, provide a variety of safe, stable surfaces such as carpets, mats, and crash pads to help students build confidence.

Wheels Station: Equipment Choices

Gym scooters, Roller Racers, and even roller skates are high-interest "wheels." While observing students at the wheels station, note which equipment draws their attention. Also note what they do with the "wheels."

- Large, long scooters provide opportunities for a variety of riding positions. Large scooters also give students the chance to ride back to back with a classmate.
- Students love to hold a rope or hoop during scooter rides. Make sure they take turns being the rider and the puller. Encircling the student a couple of times with a coop band (a stretch band covered with polar fleece) provides some pressure while being pulled (figure 7.15).
- The go-go pedaler is a unique wheeled item that is very popular (figure 7.16).

FIGURE 7.15 Using a coop band with a scooter can provide pressure that students like along with fulfilling their interest in wheels.

FIGURE 7.16 Student checks out a new piece of balance equipment before he tries to stand on the go-go pedaler.

Vestibular Stimulation (Rocking, Spinning, and Swinging): Equipment Choices

Rocking, spinning, and swinging are all movements that help to calm students. Rocking causes the release of endorphins. Often, students come to the gym and spin in place or around the gym. Others stand and rock back and forth. Note these behaviors in your informal assessment. While engaging with students on equipment at this station, model or assist them with a variety of movements and positions.

- Video chairs provide an opportunity to rock and engage in assisted sit-ups at the same time.
- A giant-sized lazy Susan on an upholstered board makes a great customized spinning platform where students can spin prone on their tummies. For standing spinners, try Spooner Boards or Duck Walkers.
- Swings can be suspended in the gym from sturdy brackets or fixtures and removed when not in use (figure 7.17). These provide opportunities for swinging and spinning.

FIGURE 7.17 A suspended swing is attached to a horizontal ladder for the student who enjoys swinging or spinning.

HELPFUL HINTS AND MODIFICATIONS

Carefully install hardware for swings. Check with appropriate officials regarding safety.

Pressure and Massage: Equipment Choices

Many students with ASD like pressure. These are the students you find trying to wiggle themselves into a stack of mats or under the cushions of a sofa. Observe students as they use the balls, bolsters, and mats at this station. Note their equipment interest. One way to provide students with pressure during the engagement part of the lesson is to roll bolsters or balls over them.

- Stability balls and bolsters can provide deep pressure and a sense of relaxation.
- Massagers are very useful as a cool-down at the end of class.
- Mats, bolsters, fitness balls, and beanbag chairs all make great things to roll over students lying on folding mats.
- Body support activities such as wheelbarrows over bolsters, hanging on or crossing horizontal ladders and climbing walls, and stall bars all provide good outlets for pressure seekers (figure 7.18).

FIGURE 7.18 A climbing wall provides an outlet for a pressure seeker.

- Weight machines offer safe and controlled activities. The weights provide pressure to students' joints as they go through the full range of movement. Weight machines are safer than free, or hand, weights because there are no weights to drop or throw. Many pieces of equipment include visual task cards with information on what to do.

Jumping and Bouncing: Equipment Choices

Jump up on, jump down, jump over, jump repeatedly, jump high—these are the skills you should note during the initial observation phase of the lesson. No jumping? Try to engage the student, perhaps with a little bouncing. Many students with ASD love to jump and bounce, which provides a great energy outlet.

- Jogging tramps are common in gyms and fitness areas. Students can jump, run in place, jump off and land on a mat, or bounce on their bottoms. Community recreation outings to gymnastics centers are frequently used as culminating activities to gymnastics units; trampolines are favorite activities at these centers.

- Pogo sticks are great outlets for jumpers! For students under 90 pounds (41 kg), try a suspended Air Pogo. Students can bounce in a seated or standing position without fear of falling.

- Hippity Hops and fitness balls make great seated bouncing surfaces. Giant-sized fitness balls can even be used in partner activities.

- Jump ropes, hoops, cone hurdles, and jump bands provide opportunities for jumping practice.

Play Skill and Social Interaction Activities

Play skills such as getting and changing partners, taking turns, waiting for a turn, and entering and exiting a game or small-group activity must be specifically taught to students with ASD. These are not skills that they can just "pick up" or learn by watching others. They need to be explicitly taught and should be considered prerequisite skills. The absence of these play skills is problematic in physical education, recess, and other social settings. For example, a simple direction such as "Get a partner" can cause great anxiety in students with ASD who have no idea what to do. A teacher may assume that the student is not complying with directions, when in fact, she has simply not been given a direction she knows how to follow. Simple directions such as this do not indicate exactly what to do; teachers need to tell students explicitly, step by step, what to do when they say "Get a partner."

The set of activities in this section focuses on small-group interactions in a parallel or associative play format. The equipment may have some interesting features (holes in the stomp rockets and ball launchers), but it is primarily selected because it seems to have the power to draw kids to it; hence the term *kid magnet*. Tag sticks with fuzzy gloves, stomp rockets that use human jumping power to send rockets flying across the playground or football field, stompers that send tennis balls into the air—these are examples of kid magnets. Because of these high-interest features, such equipment draws kids to the activity, greatly enhancing their chances of interacting and playing together. Some activities provide assistance and visual structure for teaching the skills needed to play, such as getting a partner or playing chase, tag, or catch. Others provide structure in a sequence giving students clear participation roles.

Get a Partner: Zoo Pals

This activity uses Zoo Pal plates to give students a visual way to find partners. Many students with ASD have very good matching skills, and this activity makes use of that strength. Students match the Zoo Pal plates to find partners.

Motor Skill Objectives   Match plates to identify a partner or group.

Age Range   Preschool, primary (K-2), intermediate (3-5).

Social Skill Objectives   Getting a partner, greeting a partner, changing partners.

Equipment and Materials Needed   Zoo Pal paper plates. These come in a variety of animals; you can also use sport-related plates (see figure 7.19).

FIGURE 7.19   Zoo Pal plates help students use matching skills to find partners.

PROCEDURE

Preselect pairs of plates (two monkeys, two frogs, two flamingos) so there is one plate for each student; make sure you have an even number of players. Place the plates upside down in a circle in the center of the gym. Have students move around the circle of plates, and on a signal, ask them each to get one plate and look at the picture. Say, "What animal are you looking for? Hold your plate up high so others can see your animal. Look around and find the person with the matching plate. Walk to that person." Model partner introductions for students: "Our plates match. We are partners." "Hi, my name is Brady." "Hi, my name is Sean." Give the partners a specific, short, easy task to do such as walking and talking during one lap around the gym, jumping up and down 10 times, or playing partner tag (see next activity). At the end, ask them to say, "Thank you for being my partner" and to return their plates upside down to the center circle. Repeat this several times. This is a nice, concrete way to visually represent partners. As students learn to get and accept different partners, you can substitute pieces of equipment to form partnerships or groups; students can match beanbags, clothespins, ball colors, or catching net and ball colors.

HELPFUL HINTS AND MODIFICATIONS

- Select plates that reflect student interests: dinosaurs, crustaceans, amphibians, and so on. Party stores have large assortments of character plates.
- Use different numbers of matching plates to organize students into small groups of three or four.
- Use the plates to change the size of student groups: Match by amphibians or match by plates that have bumps like the eyes of a frog, flamingo feet, or monkey ears.
- If you are a special education teacher and are reinforcing the social skill of introductions, use the same scripts and procedures you use in the regular classroom in physical education class.

Tag, You're It!

Tag, You're It! helps students learn how to play the game of tag with the help of visual cues.

Motor Skill Objectives Chasing and fleeing, adjusting to small-organization games.

Age Range Preschool, primary (K-2), intermediate (3-5).

Social Skill Objectives Assuming the role of "tagger" in a game.

Equipment and Materials Needed A tag stick (see appendix 7E for directions for building a tag stick), tagging hand, foam noodle, or thunder stick can supply the extra visual cue to help students with ASD understand the "it" in tag games (see figure 7.20). The idea is to make the tagger visually obvious and to teach the student with ASD what to do as the tagger.

FIGURE 7.20 A tag stick helps students identify who is "it."

PROCEDURE

Have students practice tagging in partners. Be very explicit and demonstrate the rules for tag in your gym or on the playground. Include such instructions as, "Where can you tag?" and identify specific body parts that students can tag such as the shoulder, back, or arm. Do not tell them where *not* to tag. Students with ASD generally have difficulty with negative instructions. Explicitly instruct students in *how* to tag with the tag stick and demonstrate what you want them to do. Check for understanding by saying, "Show me how to tag." Help them to get the right touch with the proper amount of force. Once they have the tagging down, have them play partner tag. One partner should be an adult or experienced peer who has the tag stick and models what to do, saying, "Tag, you're it. Your turn [while handing the student the tag stick]. Come get me." Gradually increase the size of the group playing tag. Assign student with ASD the role of tagger along with three or four peers who can assist them.

HELPFUL HINTS AND MODIFICATIONS

- Students with ASD can be made "all-time tagger," meaning that their job in the game is *only* to tag.
- Teach freeze tag, instructing students to stop and freeze when they are touched by the tag stick.
- Teach students how to reenter the game. Tunnel tag is a good example. Say, "Freeze in a straddle stance until someone crawls between your legs."
- Have students use a variety of locomotor patterns in tag games.

Throw, Throw, Throw, . . . Catch, Catch, Catch

This is a game of throwing and catching that gives students a chance to practice the drill. Once established, it can be used in a number of settings with a variety of objects across many physical education units.

Motor Skill Objectives   Tossing and catching a variety of balls and objects, object projection force and accuracy, object reception.

Age Range   Preschool, primary (K-2), intermediate (3-5), middle school (6-8), high school (9-12), 18+.

Social Skill Objectives   Turn taking.

Equipment and Materials Needed   Frisbees and flying rings, buckets for the equipment and lots of balls, beanbags, deck tennis rings, fishing dip nets and catching nets, beanbags, rebound nets, and tchoukball nets. Appendix 7F has directions for making nets or cooperative catchers.

PROCEDURE

Select items to be tossed and caught based on student interest or your instructional unit. Begin throwing and catching instruction using objects that don't roll away, such as beanbags. Start with 10 to 20 objects to throw and catch. If students are not proficient catchers, have them use a fishing dip net or catching net to ensure catching success. If your student tends to wander away from activities, have him sit down on the floor or on a fitness ball. If distractions are an issue, have him face a corner of the gymnasium, which cuts down the visual field. Hand the student a catching net and say, "Hold." Begin to toss beanbags one at a time into the catching net, saying "Catch" prior to each toss. Say, "Catch, Catch" until all the objects have been thrown. Dump the beanbags into a bucket or on the floor next to the student. Provide specific instructions such as, "Dean's turn to throw" and "Ms. Ann's turn to catch." Give the student a beanbag and hold the catching net while giving him throwing instructions. Repeat until all of the beanbags are back in the catching net. Once the student has the pattern of throwing, throw, throw, . . . catch, catch, catch, change the items used. Try bouncing tennis balls into the catching net, or tossing Frisbees or flying discs. Try the throwing-and-catching pattern without the catching net, asking students to catch with their hands.

HELPFUL HINTS AND MODIFICATIONS

- Have students work in pairs using a catching net. Partners share a catching hoop, holding opposite sides of the hoop. They move together to catch balls. The partner can help get the student with ASD into the catching position by moving to the ball.
- Use a pitch-back net or tchoukball rebound net to teach throwing and catching.
- Use washable beanbags filled with plastic pellets.

Cardboard Tube Car Tunnels

Cardboard Tube Car Tunnels incorporates the turn-ons of black holes and wheels described earlier. Students roll cars down the tube to a friend or to knock over pins.

Motor Skill Objectives   Rolling to a target, rolling cars with a partner.

Age Range   Preschool, primary (K-2), intermediate (3-5), middle school (6-8).

Social Skill Objectives Parallel play with turn taking.

Equipment and Materials Needed A cardboard tube for each player recycled from a carpet store or recycled from a large laminating machine, and small toy cars (see figure 7.21). Tubes range in length from 3 to 6 feet (1 to 2 m).

PROCEDURE

Partners are seated facing each other. Each has a tube, and one partner has a tub containing a number of cars. The partner with the cars begins to roll them down the tube one at a time. As each car arrives, the other partner rolls it down her tube to return it to her partner. This sets up a perpetual car flow helping to sustain play.

HELPFUL HINTS AND MODIFICATIONS

Have partners roll cars down the tube to knock over empty pop cans or metal energy juice bottles. They make great, noisy, inexpensive pins!

FIGURE 7.21 Students roll the small toy cars down the tube to practice rolling to a target.

Stomp Rockets

Students place rockets on the launcher and either stomp or jump to launch them. Rockets are retrieved and launched again. This is a high-interest activity that is easy to structure into a small-group turn-taking activity. The activity is presented in two parts: learning to launch and launching with friends.

Motor Skill Objectives Stomping with force, jumping, motor planning.

Age Range Primary (K-2), intermediate (3-5), middle school (6-8), high school (9-12), 18+.

Social Skill Objectives Turn taking.

Equipment and Materials Needed Ultra Stomp Rockets can be used outside or in large indoor spaces. Foam Stomp Rocket Jr. can be used indoors or with younger students (see figure 7.22).

PROCEDURE

Part 1: Learning to launch (one stomp rocket launcher and three rockets per student).
Students load and launch each of the rockets and then retrieve all three. At the cue "Rocket on," the student slides the hollow rocket onto the end of the rocket launcher. Model and say, "Stomp." Student may stomp or jump on the pink pad to launch the rocket. When teaching students to load and launch the rockets, provide at least three trials in a row. Students retrieve the rockets to repeat the activity.

Part 2: Launching with friends. Once students know how to load, launch, and retrieve the rockets, place three poly spots by each stomp rocket launch pad to indicate where to wait for a turn. Player 1 loads and stomps and runs to retrieve the rocket; then player 2 loads, stomps, and retrieves, and player 3 is up. As players return with rockets, they wait on the spots, moving up as the person in front stomps and moves to retrieve. This creates a perpetual flow of fun.

HELPFUL HINTS AND MODIFICATIONS

- Use poly spots to indicate the number of players per station (figure 7.22). Use the same number of poly spots as you have rockets for each stomp rocket station. Three poly spots = three students, each with a rocket.

- Have students play on a football field so you can measure the distance of the launch.

- When launching outdoors, vertical shots are lots of fun.

FIGURE 7.22 Stomp Rockets helps students with taking turns.

Funnel Shooters and Catching Nets

Students work together to launch and catch balls. This is a small-group activity requiring five people: three to shoot and two to catch.

Motor Skill Objectives   Cooperation, catching with a net or hands, problem solving.

Age Range   Intermediate (3-5), middle school (6-8), high school (9-12), 18+.

Social Skill Objectives   Peer interaction and cooperation, changing jobs in a cooperative task.

Equipment and Materials Needed   Funnel shooters, poly spots (numbered 1 through 5), and a large quantity of items to launch (e.g., yarn balls, beanbags, tennis balls). For outdoor fun, try water balloons. TeamLaunchers, TeamKatchers, and MyKatchers are commercially available from Sportime. Directions for making your own catching nets or cooperative catchers and funnel shooters are in appendixes 7F and 7G.

PROCEDURE

The funnel shooter requires three people to operate: one launcher and two holders. It is helpful to number the positions with numbered poly spots so students understand the rotation. The objective is to launch objects cooperatively. Holders hold the handles of the launcher and face the target. The launcher places a beanbag in the funnel, pulls down and back, and releases. Give students 10 trials before they rotate positions in numbered order (1 goes to 2, 2 goes to 3, and so on). Catchers are in the field and may catch with hands, mitts, or catching nets.

HELPFUL HINTS AND MODIFICATIONS

- Use yarn balls and beanbags inside and when learning to operate the funnel shooter.
- Dead tennis balls are available in large supply from tennis clubs and teams and work well for outdoor launching and catching.
- Water balloons can be used during warm weather.

Stomp and Catch

Stomp and Catch is essentially as the name describes. Students use stomp ball launchers to launch tennis balls to classmates who are attempting to catch, or field, them. This is another novel piece of equipment that incites students' curiosity and makes them want to join the activity.

Motor Skill Objectives   Stomping or jumping to put a ball into play, motor planning, catching or gathering balls.

Age Range   Primary (K-2), intermediate (3-5), middle school (6-8), high school (9-12), 18+.

Social Skill Objectives   Turn taking, changing roles, partner work, choice making.

Equipment and Materials Needed

Launching: Stomp ball launchers, one for every two or three students; one bucket or basket of tennis balls per launcher.

Retrieving: Provide a selection of items for catching and retrieving: catching net, tennis ball picker-uppers, or tennis ball baskets. Make sure there is at least one item per student in the field. Make a catching net or cooperative catcher (see appendix 7F) or use a fishing dip net or commercially available products such as MyKatchers or TeamKatchers.

PROCEDURE

This activity provides students with a number of jobs or roles to perform using a variety of interesting and fun equipment. Teach equipment use. To launch, the student takes a tennis ball from the basket or bucket, places it in the hole of the ball launcher, pushes it all the way in, and stomps or jumps on the launcher to send the ball flying. Stompers stomp until all of the balls in the basket are gone; then they move to the field to catch or gather.

Balls can be caught in catching nets, caught with the hands, or picked up with tennis ball picker-uppers. Teach students with catching nets to hold the net or hoop and pick up or catch tennis balls. The tennis ball picker-upper requires students to place the tube on the ball and push down. Explain that the ball needs to go *in* the tube. When the tube is full, they turn it upside down and pour the balls into the bucket or laundry basket. Students can also collect tennis balls with the tennis basket. It is designed to be placed on top of the tennis ball and pushed down. The ball moves through the bottom of the basket and is easily collected. Then the ball goes into the basket. Assign students to the roles of stompers and retrievers. Retrievers or catchers may change equipment during their turns, from tennis ball picker-uppers to tennis ball baskets to catching nets.

HELPFUL HINTS AND MODIFICATIONS

- Use the ball stompers outdoors on the tennis court. Students on one side of the court stomp tennis balls across the net. Students on the other side of the net get lots of practice returning stomped balls with tennis rackets.
- Add a tennis ball shooter to the lesson. Students launch, catch or pick up the ball, and reload the hopper! This increases the speed of launching, which increases the challenge for the retrievers.
- Rapid fire challenge: Tell students: "Stomp all the balls as fast as you can."
- Football fields are great places to measure the distance stomped!

Motor and Sport Skill Stations

Students with ASD need lots of practice to develop motor and sport skills. Stations in this section provide choice, a variety of tasks and equipment, and active participation with a focus on positive practice. A variety of equipment and station activities relate to motor and sport skills and include visual cues and unique equipment uses. These activities facilitate instruction and fun for students with ASD and can enhance instruction for *all* students.

Baseball or Softball Station Suggestions

Throw to Target

In this activity students practice their throwing skills using yarn balls as a lead-up to throwing baseballs or softballs. Accuracy is tested by provided a target for students to throw to.

Motor Skill Objectives   Overhand throw, throwing force and accuracy.

Age Range   Primary (K-2), intermediate (3-5), middle school (6-8), high school (9-12), 18+; readily adaptable to any age group.

Social Skill Objectives   Turn taking.

Equipment and Materials Needed   Duct tape, two hula hoops if available, 5-gallon bucket or container with yarn balls (10 to 20).

PROCEDURE

Tape the hula hoops to the gym wall to provide a target zone roughly waist high (strike zone). Place poly spots or footprints a distance from the target, and provide a bucket of yarn balls to throw. Ask students to step and throw to the target on the wall. Model by saying, "Step and throw" as you throw the yarn ball to the target or hoop. Repeat. Wait for the student to throw. Offer a ball. Take another ball and model stepping and throwing again. Assist as necessary. Give students 10 trials before changing stations. Adjust the throwing distance from the target based on each student's ability (see figure 7.23).

FIGURE 7.23   *(a)* Equipment used in this activity and *(b)* a student throws the ball to the target on the wall.

HELPFUL HINTS AND MODIFICATIONS

- Have students use beanbags for throwing. They do not roll away and are easy to gather.
- Change equipment as student age increases. Begin with beanbags in elementary school, switching to rag or mush softballs in middle and high school. Yarn balls, if available, are great at all levels. When thrown hard, they fly true to the target and do not rebound too rapidly or hurt anyone.
- Use beanbags called slammers that make a sound when thrown at the target: "Hey Hey!"
- If hoops are unavailable, duct tape Xs to the wall as targets. Colorful duct tape increases attention!
- Increase the distance to the target as skill levels improve. Move the poly spots or footprints back.
- Use a moving target. Rather than taping the hoop to the wall, tie a rope to a hoop and tape the rope to the wall so the hoop swings from the rope.

Baseball or Softball Station Suggestions
Batting Practice With Zip-N-Hit

The Zip-N-Hit provides a great way to practice batting. The ball is "pitched" along a string, and the batter swings the Wiffle bat or flat bat along the string to return the ball to the pitcher, providing lots of practice time with no need to chase the ball. This activity can be set up indoors or outdoors.

Motor Skill Objectives   Object interception, striking.

Age Range   Intermediate (3-5), middle school (6-8), high school (9-12).

Social Skill Objectives   Cooperation, changing roles (pitcher, batter).

Equipment and Materials Needed   Zip-N-Hit Pitching Machine (uses a Wiffle ball), Zip-N-Hit Pro, Wiffle bat, flat bat, or foam bat.

PROCEDURE

Using a door handle, bleacher banister, pole, or other available anchor, attach the clip end of the Zip-N-Hit around the anchor. One student pitches by holding the handles of the Zip-N-Hit and moving his arms apart. The ball slides down the string to another student, who returns the ball to the pitcher by swinging the bat along the string. Zip-N-Hit is commercially available at sporting goods stores.

HELPFUL HINTS AND MODIFICATIONS

- For outdoor use, attach the Zip-N-Hit to a fence or backstop.
- A DVD comes with the Zip-N-Hit Pro and provides a good preview of operation.
- Students may "throw" (slide) the ball back to the pitcher, rather than hit it with a bat.

Batting and Base Running With Blast Ball

Blast ball, a great entry-level game, is a one-base baseball game. The game is played with a foam ball, foam bat, batting tee, and one base that honks when stepped on (see figure 7.24). Students bat the ball into play. The ball is considered to be in play when it passes the fair play line (yellow strap with weighted ends). The batter runs to the base, stepping on it to make it honk. Fielder(s) attempt to catch the ball and yell "Blast" before the runner gets to first. Blast ball equipment is used here in a two-student station to teach students to hit the ball and run to the base.

Motor Skill Objectives Batting, base running.

Age Range Primary (K-2), intermediate (3-5).

Social Skill Objectives Turn taking.

Equipment and Materials Needed Batting tee; Wiffle, flat, or fat bat; 5-gallon bucket with 6 to 15 Wiffle balls; poly spots; hula hoop; blast ball base.

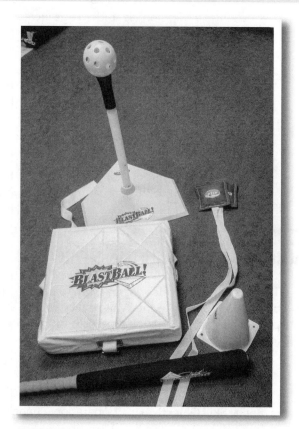

FIGURE 7.24 Students practice batting and base running in this activity.

PROCEDURE

Set the batting tee on a floor line. Place the blast ball base about 25 feet (7.6 m) away, down the line. Place the Wiffle balls in the bucket next to the batting tee. Use the poly spots to indicate foot placement for the batter (adjusting for left- and right-handed batters). Place the hula hoop to provide a safe on-deck circle in which the next batter can wait. Bats can be placed in the hoop to give students a choice of equipment. Model the routine: "Pick up a bat, place the ball on the tee, stand on the spots, swing at [or hit] the ball, run to the base, HONK, back to the hula hoop [or on-deck circle], wait for John to bat, and then do it again!" Assist as necessary. Plan to have each student bat and run about five times before changing stations.

HELPFUL HINTS AND MODIFICATIONS

- This tends to be a "love it" or "hate it" activity for students with ASD. Many love that the base honks when they step on it. A few students *hate* the sound of the base. Provide noise-cancelling headphones if this happens, or substitute a base that does not honk.
- Play the game outdoors to diminish the sound of the base.
- Provide an adjustable-height batting tee.
- Set the ball on the tee for the student if needed.

Hit and Run

This activity provides practice using batting tees to hit a ball and then running around the bases.

Motor Skill Objectives   Striking, base running.

Age Range   Intermediate (3-5), middle school (6-8), high school (9-12).

Social Skill Objectives   Turn taking.

Equipment and Materials Needed   A variety of bats (fat bats, flat bats, Wiffle bats, foam bats); a batting tee; a choice of balls (Wiffle balls, colored balls, foam balls, rag balls) in a bucket or basket; four indoor bases or poly spots; numbered cones or poly spots.

PROCEDURE

Set the four bases in a small diamond formation in a corner or quarter of the gym. Place home plate, or cone 4, diagonally across from the corner (second base). This uses the walls and floor lines as natural boundaries and baselines. Place numbered cones next to the bases (cone 1 at first, cone 2 at second, and so on). Cone 4 should also say "Home" because the direction "Run home" can be very confusing to students who are very literal in their interpretation of language.

HELPFUL HINTS AND MODIFICATIONS

- Provide batting tees at a variety of heights.
- Make a batting tee for a larger ball using a funnel or plunger. Place the funnel or plunger in the hole of a traffic cone.

Ball Handling

Task cards and DVDs for basketball skills are available in many physical education curricular guides. Use the pictures and photos on the task cards as well as the instructional video tips to help students acquire ball-handling skills.

Motor Skill Objectives   Ball handling, dribbling.

Age Range   Primary (K-2), intermediate (3-5), middle school (6-8), high school (9-12); readily adaptable to all ages.

Social Skill Objectives   Turn taking.

Equipment and Materials Needed   Basketballs (junior size for young students), deck tennis rings (one per ball), cones, task cards, TV/DVD player, instructional DVD.

PROCEDURE

Set up a station with basketballs and a number of activity task cards. Place the basketballs on deck tennis rings to hold them in place. Students follow the task cards or video clip to practice ball-handling skill. Provide a pathway of cones through which students can dribble the ball. Make sure there is at least one task at each station that all students can do (e.g., ball taps, ball spin). Provide challenging tasks as well.

HELPFUL HINTS AND MODIFICATIONS

- If available, use the skill or task cards from the game Basketball Skillastics. Skillastics games provide 26 sport-related skills with task cards.
- SPARK physical education curricular materials provide a number of task cards for students of many ages.
- Allow "air ball" practice, in which students practice the movement without a ball (e.g., dribbling, figure eights).
- Provide a variety of sizes, weights, and textures of basketballs. Use giant-sized balls or slower-moving Gertie balls. Hold balls in position at the station with hoops or deck tennis rings.

Basketball Station Suggestions

Bounce Pass

When teaching passing to a partner, begin by teaching the bounce pass. The bounce gives students additional time and an auditory cue to prepare to catch.

Motor Skill Objectives   Chest pass, bounce pass to a partner, catch.

Age Range   Intermediate (3-5), middle school (6-8), high school (9-12).

Social Skill Objectives   Turn taking, cooperation.

Equipment and Materials Needed   Basketballs (small or intermediate [junior] size for younger, smaller students), other balls that bounce, poly spots, indoor base, deck tennis rings or hoops to hold the balls in place.

PROCEDURE

Place a variety of balls in hoops or on deck tennis rings to give students choices at the station. Place two poly spots about 10 feet (3 m) apart. Adjust the distance based on student skill. Place an indoor base between the two poly spots, providing a target for the bounce pass. Partners select one of the balls to play catch with and stand on each of the poly spots. Demonstrate the chest pass and position. Cue students to keep "Elbows up" and to "Step and push," bouncing the ball on or near the base. Prompt the student receiving the ball to keep "Hands up" and ready to catch. One student steps and bounces (using a two-handed chest pass) the basketball onto the base. The partner catches and returns the pass. Students shoot for a minimum of 10 trials before stopping.

HELPFUL HINTS AND MODIFICATIONS

- If students tend to move off the spot, have them sit on a fitness ball to play catch.
- Initially, students may need to play catch with a skilled peer or adult.
- Have students practice with a pitch-back net.
- Once students are proficient with the bounce pass, have them try the chest pass with a partner.

Shooting

Students practice their shooting skills in this activity with different types of balls and targets.

Motor Skill Objectives   Object projection and accuracy, shooting.

Age Range   Primary (K-2), intermediate (3-5), middle school (6-8), high school (9-12); readily adaptable to all ages.

Social Skill Objectives   Turn taking.

Equipment and Materials Needed   A variety of balls and basketballs, deck tennis rings, hula hoops.

PROCEDURE

Provide developmentally appropriate equipment (junior balls for young students). Balls can be held in position at the shooting station with deck tennis rings, giant rings, or hula hoops. Students shoot baskets at this station. Have them use a variety of baskets or targets such as hula hoops duct taped together and hung over the rim.

HELPFUL HINTS AND MODIFICATIONS

- Use "hands-on" basketballs that show hand positions for shooting baskets.
- Use hula hoops as giant-sized baskets.
- Use adjustable-height hoops such as Hang a Hoop.
- Use TeamKatchers or MyKatcher catching nets as baskets.
- Hang a hoop over the rim of a basketball hoop; students earn 2 points for the basket and 1 point if the ball goes through the hoop.
- Have students play HORSE or any other word you want to spell.
- Use poly spots to indicate shooting positions for Around the World.
- Use commercially available Hot Shot shooting spots.
- Scatter numbered poly spots around the court; students who make baskets from poly spots earn the number of points on the poly spot.

Punting

Punting is a difficult skill that requires timing and coordination. Lack of success with this skill leads to disinterest or frustration. Using a suspended football provides opportunities for repeated practice and success.

Motor Skill Objectives   Eye–foot coordination, kicking, punting.

Age Range   Primary (K-2), intermediate (3-5), middle school (6-8), high school (9-12).

Social Skill Objectives   Turn taking.

Equipment and Materials Needed   Footballs (foam, gripper, or Wiffle), a nylon stocking for each football. Provide about two balls per student.

PROCEDURE

Create a suspended football punting station by using a nylon stocking or a commercially available tethered football (figure 7.25). Simply slide the football into one end of the stocking to make a "boomerang" football. You or an assistant can hold the tether and model the kick for the student. Students may also hold the tether and kick. The tethered football could be suspended from a basketball rim. This activity provides students with repeated practice and limited chase time.

HELPFUL HINTS AND MODIFICATIONS

- Wiffle footballs can be suspended with cord from a basketball rim or backstop.
- Many football-shaped dog toys come with a tether that can be used to suspend them.
- Make the skill easier to perform by using a giant-sized Omnikin football.
- Provide a couple of untethered footballs at the station for students who are ready for the challenge of dropping and kicking.

FIGURE 7.25 Students practice punting and kicking the footballs to help them work on eye–foot coordination.

Football Station Suggestions

Passing and Receiving

Teamed with a skilled partner or adult, students play catch using a variety of footballs. Slo-Mo Bump, pebble, and gripper footballs are easy to catch. Giant-sized Omnikin footballs are fun to try to pass and catch. A Throton, which is a plastic device with two cones, encourages a great spiral throw. They are also hollow, which makes them interesting (black holes). Using fun and relatively softer football equipment helps keep students interested in play.

Motor Skill Objectives   Object projection, catching, passing.

Age Range   Intermediate (3-5), middle school (6-8), high school (9-12).

Social Skill Objectives   Turn taking, cooperation.

Equipment and Materials Needed   A variety of footballs (Slo-Mo Bump, pebble, gripper, Omnikin, Throtons, Vortex Howlers); hoop; poly spots.

PROCEDURE

Place a variety of footballs in the hoop at the station. Set up two sets of spots about 10 feet (3 m) apart. Ask the student to select a football and stand on or near a spot. You or a partner models the throwing motion, saying to the student, "Step, throw." Wait for the student to step and throw and then catch or retrieve the ball. Model for the student "Hands up, ready to catch," and then toss the ball back. Continue playing catch. Try a variety of footballs.

HELPFUL HINTS AND MODIFICATIONS

- Have students practice throwing footballs to a hoop on the wall; use footprints to indicate foot placement.
- Adjust the throwing distance as necessary.

Football Station Suggestions
Kicking Tees

Students practice taking turns kicking a football. They learn to follow directions and learn the developmental steps needed for this skill.

Motor Skill Objectives   Eye–foot coordination, kicking, punting.

Age Range   Primary (K-2), intermediate (3-5), middle school (6-8), high school (9-12).

Social Skill Objectives   Turn taking.

Equipment and Materials Needed   Five footballs, five kicking tees, five footprints or poly spots.

PROCEDURE

Place each football on a kicking tee along a line, spacing the tees 2 or 3 feet (about 1 m) apart. Place a footprint or poly spot next to each kicking tee. Model the action while saying, "Step" (placing your foot on the poly spot), "kick" (kicking the ball to the wall), and "Nate's turn" (use the student's name).

HELPFUL HINTS AND MODIFICATIONS

- Use deck tennis rings if kicking tees are not available. Simply stand the football in the deck tennis ring.
- Have students try kicking with both the right foot and the left foot. Move the poly spot accordingly (place it to the left of the tee for a right-legged kick and to the right of the tee for a left-legged kick).

Soccer Station Suggestions
Kicking

In this activity, students learn how to kick to a target and reset the equipment. They kick balls from the deck tennis rings to the bowling pins (figure 7.26).

Motor Skill Objectives   Eye–foot coordination, shooting.

Age Range   Primary (K-2), intermediate (3-5), middle school (6-8), high school (9-12).

Social Skill Objectives   Turn taking.

Equipment and Materials Needed   Equal numbers of soccer balls, deck tennis rings, and bowling pins.

FIGURE 7.26   Students kick balls from the deck tennis rings to the bowling pins to work on eye–foot coordination.

PROCEDURE

Set up the bowling pins along a line about 3 feet (1 m) apart. Set a soccer ball on a deck tennis ring about 10 feet (3 m) in front of each pin. Model while saying, "Step, kick." Students kick each of the balls to the pins. Pins are reset. Balls are retrieved and replaced in the deck tennis rings. Now say, "Do it again."

HELPFUL HINTS AND MODIFICATIONS

- Use a variety of soccer balls (e.g., pebble soccer balls, gripper balls, indoor soccer balls, Kixz balls, soccer Omnikin balls).
- Increase the distance from the pins as students' skills increase.
- Place pins on poly spots rather than on a line.

Soccer Station Suggestions
Ball Handling With Boomerang Balls or Soccer Pals

Soccer Pals are commercially available individual training aids for novice through elite athletes. The soccer ball is held in a net on a tether to provide the student with repeated practice. Using nylon hose and foam balls or soccer balls, you can make your own trainers, which are also known as boomerang balls because they come back. Students practice ball-handling skills without ever losing control of the ball.

Motor Skill Objectives Eye–foot coordination, ball handling.

Age Range Primary (K-2), intermediate (3-5), middle school (6-8), high school (9-12).

Social Skill Objectives Turn taking.

Equipment and Materials Needed Soccer balls (about four; select size and weight according to student size), one Soccer Pal or nylon stocking per soccer ball, hoop or crate to hold the trainers.

PROCEDURE

Stretch the hose over the soccer ball to make a boomerang ball, or place a soccer ball in a Soccer Pal. Place the trainers in the hoop or crate at the station. Select a trainer, hold the end of the hose or trainer, and model a variety of ball skills (e.g., taps, kicks). Hand one to the student, saying "Kick."

HELPFUL HINTS AND MODIFICATIONS

Suspend the soccer ball from a basketball hoop.

Soccer Station Suggestions
Shoot! Goal, Goal, Goal

Students learn how to shoot a goal and practice accuracy. They are provided with goals and learn a cue to use when kicking the ball.

Motor Skill Objectives Eye–foot coordination, shooting.

Age Range Primary (K-2), intermediate (3-5), middle school (6-8), high school (9-12).

Social Skill Objectives Turn taking.

Equipment and Materials Needed Two small individual nets, two soccer balls per net, four deck tennis rings.

PROCEDURE

Small pop-up goals give students a place to aim their shots. Set up individual nets and place two soccer balls on deck tennis rings (see figure 7.27). Model while saying, "Kick in."

HELPFUL HINTS AND MODIFICATIONS

FIGURE 7.27 Students practice accuracy by shooting the soccer ball at their individual net.

- Vary soccer ball size and texture according to student interest.
- Vary the distance from the goal based on student ability and success.
- Have students practice outside on grass.

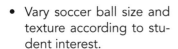

Pass to a Partner

Set up a station at which partners pass a soccer ball to each other.

Motor Skill Objectives Eye–foot coordination, shooting.

Age Range Primary (K-2), intermediate (3-5), middle school (6-8), high school (9-12).

Social Skill Objectives Turn taking.

Equipment and Materials Needed A variety of balls for kicking (e.g., soccer, Kixz balls [foam balls with holes], gripper and foam soccer balls, indoor soccer balls), hoop to contain balls, poly spots (one per student).

PROCEDURE

Set up a partner passing station with a variety of soccer balls, two poly spots, one deck tennis ring, and one ball. Partners stand on spots opposite each other (a few feet, or about a meter, to start) and pass a ball back and forth.

HELPFUL HINTS AND MODIFICATIONS

Try medicine balls for kicking activities. The heavier weight helps students to know that they have kicked something. Medicine balls (especially leather ones) tend to roll more slowly than soccer balls.

Equipment Turn-Ons

If the student is into	Try
Black holes	• Wiffle balls • Bowling balls • Billiard tables • Marble mazes • Kaleidoscopes • Tubes (carpet, paper towel, plastic) • Aerobies (flying rings) • Whirlers • Funnels • Inner tubes • Putting greens with holes • Deck tennis rings • Hoops
Wheels	• Tricycles or bicycles • Tandem bikes • Scooters • Wagons • Stationery bikes • Wheelercisers • Riding trucks • Roller skates or inline skates • Roller Racers • Skateboards • Scooters
Strings	• String nets (volleyball, badminton, and basketball) • Rackets • Jump ropes • Fishing poles • Geodesic balls • Pitch-back nets • Rappelling ropes • Kites • Yo-yos • Helium balloons on strings • Koosh balls • Spider balls • Climbing ropes • Handlebar streamers • Comet balls • Lace-up skates • Zoom balls • Zip-N-Hit • Fishing dip nets • Catching nets or cooperative catchers

If the student is into	Try
Small spaces	• Boxes • Tents • Equipment carts • Tunnels • Fiber barrels • Body Sox • Pop-up cubes
Spinning	• Sit-n-Spin • Spooner boards • Dizzy Discs or Astronaut Boards • Carnival rides • Doodle Tops • Merry-go-rounds • Scooter helicopter rides • Snow tube spinning • Hammock swings • Hoops
Reaction	• Push-and-go toys • Bounce-back net • Switches • Pinball machines • Bop Bags • Squeeze noisemakers • Beanbag Silly Slammers
Jumping	• Pogo sticks • Air Pogo • Space Ball (trampoline game) • Vestibular boards • Hippity Hops • Potato sacks • Jogging tramps • Inner tubes • Cage balls • Sleds and snow tubes • Spring board (diving)
Balancing	• Balance beams and slack lines • Bicycles • Tree climbing • Stilts • Unicycles • Ladder climbing • Balance puzzles

(continued)

From M. Grenier (ed.), 2014, *Physical education for students with autism spectrum disorders: A comprehensive approach* (Champaign, IL: Human Kinetics).

If the student is into	Try
Vestibular stimulation	• Park swings • Rope swings • Hammocks • Gliders • Front porch swings • Slides • Airwalkers (suspended swings) • Elliptical machines
Tactile sensations	• Swimming • Deep pressure activities • Toys that vibrate • Squeezers • Massagers • Mat sandwich • Coop band (a stretch band covered with polar fleece) • Parachutes • Large beanbag animals • Weighted snakes, frogs • Inside-out balls • Spaghetti balls
Visual stimulation	• Tornado tubes • Glitter tubes • Rope lights • Sound-activated rope lights • Lights • Liquid or sand timers • Lightning balls (lights) • Lava lamps

Informal Assessment of Students at Stations: Younger Group

The focus of this informal assessment is to learn what objects and activities interest the learner and how the learner interacts with the provided materials. This information will be helpful in planning future activities for the learner or groups of learners.

Student: Date:

Activity	Interested?	Minutes engaged	Observations: What does he or she do?
Balls	YES or NO	Less 1 2 3 4 5 More	Identify specific balls selected by student.
Balance	YES or NO	Less 1 2 3 4 5 More	
Wheels: Scooters	YES or NO	Less 1 2 3 4 5 More	
Wheels: Roller Racers	YES or NO	Less 1 2 3 4 5 More	
Rocking and spinning: Sit and spin	YES or NO	Less 1 2 3 4 5 More	
Jumping or bouncing: Air Pogo	YES or NO	Less 1 2 3 4 5 More	
Jumping or bouncing: Jogging tramp	YES or NO	Less 1 2 3 4 5 More	
Pressure: Bolster and mat	YES or NO	Less 1 2 3 4 5 More	
Other	YES or NO	Less 1 2 3 4 5 More	
Other	YES or NO	Less 1 2 3 4 5 More	
Other	YES or NO		

Informal Assessment of Students at Stations: Older Group

The focus of this informal assessment is to learn what objects and activities interest the learner and how the learner interacts with the provided materials. This information will be helpful in planning future activities for the learner or groups of learners.

Student: Date:

Activity	Interested?	Minutes engaged	Observations: What does he or she do?
Balls: Medicine balls and bounce-back net	YES or NO	Less 1 2 3 4 5 More	
Balls: Footballs	YES or NO	Less 1 2 3 4 5 More	
Balance: Indo Balance Board	YES or NO	Less 1 2 3 4 5 More	
Wheels: Razor scooters	YES or NO	Less 1 2 3 4 5 More	
Wheels and pressure: Scooters and coop band (a stretch band covered with polar fleece)	YES or NO	Less 1 2 3 4 5 More	
Rocking and spinning: Spooner boards	YES or NO	Less 1 2 3 4 5 More	
Jumping and bouncing: Fitness balls	YES or NO	Less 1 2 3 4 5 More	
Other: Hoops	YES or NO	Less 1 2 3 4 5 More	

Ribbon Ball Station Card

- Hold on to the ball or ribbon and create movements.
- Move the ribbon ball high or low, side to side, or like a lasso; make circles to the side of the body and in front of the body; make figure eights at different heights.
- Toss the ribbon ball to a target.
- Throw the ribbon ball through a hoop.
- Move to music.
- Grab any part of the ball for movement.
- Throw over a volleyball net (this makes a nice visual arc or rainbow).

How to Build a Tag Stick

Tag Sticks

Use for ALL tag activities
Extends reach
Identifies "it"
Soft touch
Built-in hand or handle grip
Can be used as a helping hand for additional stability on a balance beam

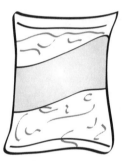

Pillow stuffing
Polyfill
Purchase at fabric stores

Duct tape, any color

Materials
1/2 in. (1 cm) foam pipe insulation
Polyfill
Duct tape
1 small glove or mitten

Stuff the glove with polyfill.
Cut pipe insulation to desired length, about 10-12 in. (25-30 cm).
Duct tape the bottom shut.
Stuff the pipe insulation with polyfill.
Duct tape the glove to the pipe insulation.

Optional: Duct tape insulation 1/2 in. (1 cm) from the sides to form a handle.
Reinforce the insulation with tape.

 From M. Grenier (ed.), 2014, *Physical education for students with autism spectrum disorders: A comprehensive approach* (Champaign, IL: Human Kinetics).

How to Build a Cooperative Catcher

Cooperative Catchers

Makes catching fun and easy.
Catch a lot of tennis balls and you have a strength activity.
Catch with a partner.
Use them inside or outside.
Catch anything, including beanbags, tennis balls, water balloons, Frisbees, or rubber chickens.

Materials
3/4 in. (2 cm) PVC black water pipe (comes in 100-ft [30.5 m] rolls)
PVC cutters
3/4 in. (2 cm) connector
Replacement fishing dip net
Popcorn kernels for sound
Hairdryer to warm PVC

Cut about 30-36 in. (76 cm-91 cm) of PVC.
Thread the dip net onto the pipe, every other loop on the PVC.
Add popcorn before you connect the ends of the PVC.

How to Build a Funnel Shooter

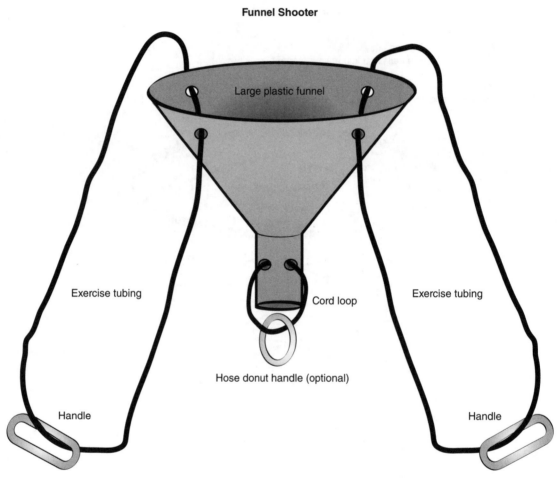

Funnel Shooter

Large plastic funnel

Exercise tubing

Cord loop

Exercise tubing

Hose donut handle (optional)

Handle

Handle

Materials
1 large plastic funnel
2 pieces of medium weight exercise tubing about 48 in. (122 cm) long (each)
2 handles (optional but helpful), 3/4 in. (2 cm) PVC or other plumbing piece
Drill with a bit that can make a large enough hole for the tubing to pass through

Drill holes, thread tubing and handle, and tie the tubing together using a square knot. Check the knot!

 From M. Grenier (ed.), 2014, *Physical education for students with autism spectrum disorders: A comprehensive approach* (Champaign, IL: Human Kinetics).

Group Games and Activities

Pat Yeaton and Michelle Grenier

This chapter includes group games and activities designed to be applied toward a lifetime of physical activity. The games are sequenced to run from elementary through high school levels to facilitate transitions between grades and ability levels. The National Association for Sport and Physical Education (NASPE) learning outcomes were used as a reference when developing the lessons to ensure consistency across content areas (NASPE, 2004).

Providing programming for challenging students is a difficult professional charge. It may take a while to assimilate students with autism spectrum disorders (ASD) into the gymnasium and class routines in a way that approximates a lesson structure. Teachers need to focus on small successful steps, followed by small-sided games. Many of the techniques necessary for the successful instruction of students with ASD are familiar to physical educators, such as using engaging equipment, routines, and repeated practice, and motivating students to learn through positive feedback. Teachers of students with ASD need to learn their individual strengths and interests and use them to engage them in physical education.

Class structure is very important in reducing anxiety. Having the students enter the gym the same way each day and establishing a predictable warm-up helps ease stress. Once students are acclimated to the gymnasium environment, physical educators can incorporate small-sided games to develop their tactical skills. Small-sided games are easily modified to minimize competition and maximize learning. Winning should never be the primary focus of the activity. Teachers would do well to emphasize cooperation, play execution, and skill development instead.

The careful selection of teams is paramount for success. Teams should be formed in consideration of personalities, skill levels, and students' ability to support their peers. Students should never be forced to work together. Teams of two to four allow for more practice opportunities in a dynamic setting.

Physical education teachers must carefully consider the skills of their students to determine whether they can accomplish the task at hand. The inclusion spectrum (outlined in chapter 3) can be used for the student with ASD to access the general physical education curriculum as the most appropriate environment. All students should have the opportunity to participate in meaningful physical education.

In this chapter, baseball and softball, basketball, flag football, floor hockey, soccer, team handball, and volleyball are presented from a developmental perspective beginning at the elementary level. The primary plans are written for elementary students at the third- to fifth-grade level, but the activities can be adapted to accommodate even younger children. Both motor skill objectives and social objectives are included so they can be used in the formation of IEP goals.

The following lessons are broken down into primary, middle, and secondary categories that include a brief description of the game, motor skill objectives and social skill objectives, equipment and materials needed, the procedure, and helpful hints and modifications.

6v6 Runaround

This game is set up to look like a real baseball diamond. There are base players and fielders and the batting team. The ball is hit off a tee, and the runner runs the bases while the fielders retrieve the ball.

Motor Skill Objectives   Striking a ball off a tee with a bat, fielding a ball, throwing and catching, running bases.

Age Range   Primary (3-5).

Social Skill Objectives   Turn taking, transitioning, cooperation.

Equipment and Materials Needed   Playing area the size of half a soccer field, batting tee, Wiffle balls, Wiffle bat, four bases, one cone.

PROCEDURE

Set up the baseball diamond inside half of the soccer field playing area. The bases should be 30 feet (9 m) apart and set up like a baseball diamond. Divide the class into teams of six. The team in the field consists of a catcher, two outfielders, and a player at each base. The batting team lines up behind a cone placed 30 feet (9 m) behind home plate. The batting tee is next to home plate. In this game the entire batting team bats before becoming fielders. The first batter hits the ball off the tee and runs to first, then to second, then to third, and finally to home plate without stopping. While the batter is running, whoever fields the ball throws it to first base. The first-base player catches the ball and throws it to second base. The second-base player catches the ball and throws it to third base. The third-base player catches the ball and throws it home to the catcher. If the batter makes it home before the catcher catches the ball and touches home plate, a run is scored. If the catcher catches the ball and touches home plate before the runner gets home, the batter does not score a run. Once everyone on the batting team has had a turn, the fielding team lines up behind the cone, ready to bat. The batting team players go out into the field to be either base players or fielders.

HELPFUL HINTS AND MODIFICATIONS

- Offer different sizes of Wiffle balls and Wiffle bats.
- Change the distance to the bases.
- Have a peer coach to help the batter navigate running the bases.
- Have a peer coach help the base player catch and throw.

Grounder Baseball

In this throwing game, a player must hit the ball off a tee, and the fielders must throw a ball around the bases.

Motor Skill Objectives   Throwing overhand to a target.

Age Range   Middle school (6-8).

Social Skill Objectives   Turn taking, transitioning, cooperating.

Equipment and Materials Needed   Bases, bats, tees, Wiffle balls or rag balls. This game can be played outside on small fields.

PROCEDURE

Divide the class into groups of five players (one batter, three infielders, and one catcher). Set up the bases as for a baseball or softball game. Play begins with a batter hitting a ball off a tee into play to one of the infielders. The batter does not run after hitting the ball. The player who catches the ball throws the ball to first base. The player at first base catches the ball and then tags the base. Now the first-base player throws the ball to second. The second-base player tags the base and throws to the third-base player, who then tags third and throws the ball home to the catcher. The batter has two ups and then becomes the first-base player. Rotate the players counterclockwise (the catcher becomes the batter).

HELPFUL HINTS AND MODIFICATIONS

- Vary the type and size of balls.
- Vary the distance between the bases.
- Create a task card that shows the location of the bases and where the batter should stand.
- Have batters run the bases. If they make it home before the ball does, they get a run. If not, they are out.

Based on Clumpner 2003.

Baseball or Softball—High School

Pitch, Hit, Run, and Field

This small-sided game includes batting and fielding.

Motor Skill Objectives   Throwing overhand, base running, lifetime leisure skills.

Age Range   High school (9-12), 18+.

Social Skill Objectives   Turn taking, transitioning, cooperating with teammates.

Equipment and Materials Needed   An area the size of half a soccer field, bases, pitching rubber, Wiffle bat, Wiffle ball.

PROCEDURE

Students are on teams of six that include a batter, a catcher, a pitcher, and three base players. The pitcher pitches to the batter; each batter receives five hits. Batter runs on the final (fifth) hit, and players determine which base to throw to, to get the batter out. Players then rotate so the pitcher becomes the catcher, the catcher becomes the batter, and the batter becomes the first-base player. The first-base player goes to second, the second-base player goes to third, and the third-base player becomes the pitcher.

HELPFUL HINTS AND MODIFICATIONS

- Create a diagram of the field with an arrow pointing to first base.
- Place diagrams on cones to indicate running directions.
- Use several sizes of plastic bats and Wiffle balls.
- Players can run only to first.

Based on Clumpner 2003.

Dribble and Roll

In this game students practice their dribbling skills. After rolling dice, students dribble the ball the number of times they roll.

Motor Skill Objectives   Dribbling a ball in general space, dribbling a ball inside a hoop.

Age Range   Primary (3-5).

Social Skill Objectives   Turn taking, cooperating, decision making.

Equipment and Materials Needed   Hula hoops, dice, playground balls or junior basketballs.

PROCEDURE

Set hula hoops around the entire gym area. Each student has a ball. On a signal, students dribble in general space until they come to a hula hoop. Once at the hoop, they stop dribbling and roll the dice. They must dribble the number they roll before moving on to the next hoop.

HELPFUL HINTS AND MODIFICATIONS

- Offer a variety of balls for students to choose from.
- Challenge students to keep dribbling while they stop to pick up the dice.

3v3

This half-court scoring game uses only passing and shooting.

Motor Skill Objectives   Chest and bounce passing, shooting at a basket, moving into appropriate position for defense and support.

Age Range   Middle school (6-8).

Social Skill Objectives   Turn taking, transitioning, cooperating.

Equipment and Materials Needed   Half a basketball court with one hoop, basketball, pinnies.

Students play a game of 3v3 basketball.

PROCEDURE

Students play five-minute 3v3 games on half a basketball court. Team must complete three consecutive passes before shooting. An attempted shot earns 1 point, and a basket earns 2 points. After each basket, players restart play at half court.

HELPFUL HINTS AND MODIFICATIONS

- Plan ahead by creating teams.
- Allow a practice time for passing and shooting before having students play this game.
- Have students count consecutive passes out loud.
- Begin with a 2v2 game and require two consecutive passes before shooting.
- Assign a peer coach to assist with play.
- Give teams specific visual plays to follow. See figure 8.1 for an example.

Based on Mitchell, Oslin, and Griffin 2006.

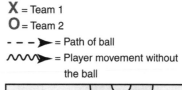

X = Team 1
O = Team 2
- - - ➤ = Path of ball
〰〰➤ = Player movement without the ball

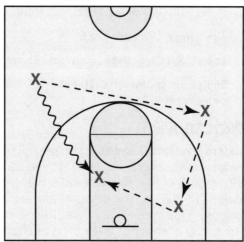

FIGURE 8.1   Sample play for teams to follow.

Basketball—High School

4v4 Half Court Jump Ball, Situational Play

In this activity, students learn how to gain possession of the ball during the jump ball.

Motor Skill Objectives   Vertical jump, tapping the ball during the vertical jump, shooting, moving into appropriate positions for support, making a successful pass under pressure, dribbling and keeping control of the ball, moving into appropriate positions for defense.

Age Range   High school (9-12), 18+.

Social Skill Objectives   Turn taking, transitioning.

Equipment and Materials Needed   Half-court playing area, pinnies, basketball.

PROCEDURE

This is a half-court 4v4 jump ball situational game in which teams attempt to win the ball by gaining possession of a jump ball. This skill can later be transferred to a basketball game. Each person on the team has a chance to do the jump ball. Teammates not part of the jump ball are taught where to stand to receive the ball from the jumper. The team that gains possession of the ball continues play until scoring or losing the ball to the opposing team. After each basket, a jump ball is called to restart the play.

HELPFUL HINTS AND MODIFICATIONS

- Plan ahead by creating teams.
- Create the opponent matchups for the jump ball.
- Model where to stand when receiving the jump ball.
- Model what to do if one's team does not win the jump ball.
- Assign a peer coach to assist with positioning.

Based on Mitchell, Oslin, and Griffin 2006.

Flag Football—Primary
3v2 Flag Football

This game involves throwing and catching a football and trying to score a touchdown. An offensive line of three players (a quarterback and two receivers) sets up against a defense of two players who guard the receivers.

Motor Skill Objectives   Passing a football, catching a football, defending against the pass.

Age Range   Primary (3-5).

Social Skill Objectives   Turn taking, transitioning, cooperating.

Equipment and Materials Needed   A quarter of a soccer field, cones for an end zone, flag belts, football.

PROCEDURE

Before students come to class, set up areas for them to play in on the soccer field. Use a quarter of the soccer field and set end zone lines 10 yards wide on each end. Divide the class into groups of five: three offensive players (one quarterback and two wide receivers) and two defensive players. The offensive players attempt to move the ball from their goal line to the opposing (defenders') goal line. The offense has three tries (downs) to get the ball to the end zone. The offense has three plays to choose from. Play cards can be laminated and given to teams to help them decide which play to use.

The quarterback chooses which play to run and makes the call. The quarterback lines up at the goal line while the receivers line up next to the quarterback. The defenders line up facing the receivers wherever they want in the field of play. The quarterback performs a quick count ("1, 2, 3, hike!") and then throws the ball to one of the wide receivers running in a pattern. If the ball is caught, the receiver runs with it toward the opposing team's end zone until his flag is pulled. While this is happening, the defense is trying to intercept the ball or grab the flag from the belt of the receiver who has caught the ball.

If a defender pulls the receiver's flag, the quarterback moves up and a second play is called from that spot (the line of scrimmage). If the ball is intercepted, the offense goes back to the goal line and has two more chances to score a touchdown. After the three chances are over, the two wide receivers switch with the two defenders; the quarterback remains to make three more plays. In the next rotation, quarterbacks switch with other students in the group of five, and this repeats until everyone has played quarterback.

HELPFUL HINTS AND MODIFICATIONS

- Create teams before class.
- Shorten the distance between the goal lines.
- Have a peer coach help players with positioning.
- Offer different sizes of footballs to accommodate all students.

Flag Football—Middle School
Running Pass Patterns

In this game, students learn a variety of pass patterns for game play.

Motor Skill Objectives   Passing a football, catching a football, understanding and performing football plays.

Age Range   Middle school (6-8).

Social Skill Objectives   Turn taking, transitioning, cooperating with teammates.

Equipment and Materials Needed   Footballs of various sizes, cones to mark team work area.

PROCEDURE

Create an area one quarter the size of a soccer field. Place cones in each corner to define the play area. Divide the class into groups of three with one quarterback and two receivers. Each team receives a play card to practice the plays (see figure 8.2). Students huddle and review and practice the play. When they can successfully execute the play, they receive a new card. Students take turns being the quarterback and receiver.

A teacher reviews the pass pattern with one of his students.

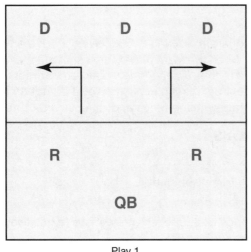

Play 1

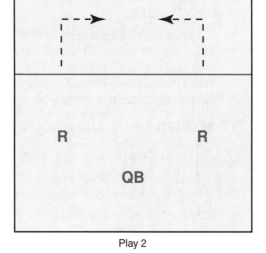

Play 2

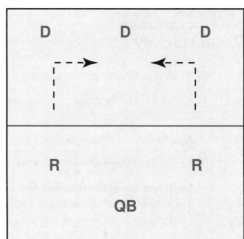

Play 3

FIGURE 8.2 Sample play cards.

HELPFUL HINTS AND MODIFICATIONS

- Plan ahead by creating teams.
- Have laminated play cards for each team.
- Assign a peer coach to assist with positioning.
- Have students remain in the same position for all of the plays.

Flag Football—High School

3v3 With a Passive Defense

In this activity, teams perform given plays with a defense that stays in position and does not try to get the ball.

Motor Skill Objectives Throwing and catching a football, performing various football plays.

Age Range High school (9-12), 18+.

Social Skill Objectives Turn taking, starting and stopping activities, cooperating with teammates.

Equipment and Materials Needed Footballs of various sizes, cones to mark the team work area (usually a quarter of a soccer field), play cards.

PROCEDURE

Students are in groups of three with one quarterback and two receivers. Each team gets a play card—a visual to use to practice the play. When the team players are confident they understand the play and have successfully completed it, they receive a new play card. Students take turns being the quarterback and receiver. Defenders remain in position and do not try to intercept the ball or touch an offensive player. Teams switch offense and defense after three plays.

HELPFUL HINTS AND MODIFICATIONS

- Plan ahead by creating teams.
- Have laminated play cards for each team (see middle school version).
- Assign a peer coach to assist with positioning.
- Have students remain in the same position for each of the plays (e.g., always the quarterback or always the receiver on the right side).

Floor Hockey—Primary

Zone Hockey

Each student plays inside a designated zone against a player from the other team.

Motor Skill Objectives Passing and receiving the puck, shooting on goal, maintaining position within a zone.

Age Range Primary (3-5).

Social Skill Objectives Turn taking, transitioning, cooperating with teammates.

Equipment and Materials Needed Floor hockey sticks, a grid marked on the gym floor with floor tape (half the gym works for primary grades), various types and sizes of balls, goals.

PROCEDURE

Divide the class into two teams and assign players to individual playing zones. Play starts with a face-off in the middle; players must stay within their zones. Sticks or feet are not allowed in other players' zones. High sticking, sticks in another zone, or feet in another zone result in players going to the penalty box for two minutes. It helps to have sticks of two different colors to distinguish teams. The object of the game is to shoot on goal to score. Goalies are assigned a safety crease, which no one else is allowed to enter.

HELPFUL HINTS AND MODIFICATIONS

- Plan ahead by creating teams.
- Assign a peer coach to assist with positioning.
- Use color-coded equipment for the teams.
- Switch students to different zones.
- Have students walk the boundaries of their zones.

Setup for Zone Hockey.

Floor Hockey—Middle School

Six-Goal Hockey

This is a modified, small-sided game of 4v4 hockey.

Motor Skill Objectives   Passing and receiving a puck.

Age Range   Middle school (6-8).

Social Skill Objectives   Turn taking, transitioning, cooperating with teammates.

Equipment and Materials Needed   Half a gym, floor hockey sticks, small cones to mark the area and larger cones to mark goals, various types and sizes of balls.

Students play a game of six-goal hockey. Note the cones placed in pairs.

PROCEDURE

Students are on teams of four with pinnies and use color-coded sticks to identify teams. Cones are placed around the gym floor inside the basketball court, in pairs, 3 feet (1 m) apart (see figure 8.3). To score (make a goal), players must shoot or pass the puck between the cones to a teammate. If the opposing team gains possession of the puck, players attempt to score by passing to a teammate between the cones. Players cannot score on the same goal twice in a row. Instead, they must dribble and pass the ball between the cones to a teammate.

HELPFUL HINTS AND MODIFICATIONS

- Plan ahead by creating teams.
- Assign a peer coach to assist with positioning.

Based on Dowson 2009.

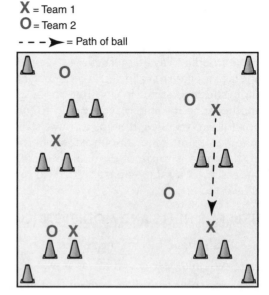

X = Team 1
O = Team 2
- - - ► = Path of ball

FIGURE 8.3 Setup for Six-Goal Hockey.

Floor Hockey—High School

3v3 Hockey and a Goalie

Students play a 3v3 game with each team having a goalie.

Motor Skill Objectives Passing and receiving, shooting on goal, supporting the puck carrier, positioning for offense and defense, goal tending.

Age Range High school (9-12), 18+.

Social Skill Objectives Turn taking, transitioning, cooperating with teammates.

Equipment and Materials Needed A quarter to half a gym area, floor hockey sticks, cones to mark goals, several types and sizes of balls or pucks.

PROCEDURE

Students are on teams of four, wearing pinnies and holding color-coded sticks. Play starts with a face-off in the middle of the play area, and players must remain as either offense or defense. Assign a goalie in the crease for safety for each team.

HELPFUL HINTS AND MODIFICATIONS

- Plan ahead by creating teams.
- Assign a peer coach to assist with positioning.
- Reduce the team size.
- Have students play two- to three-minute games, and rotate teams on and off the playing area.

4v4 Passing

In this passing game, five consecutive passes score 1 point.

Motor Skill Objectives Passing and receiving, off-the-ball movement.

Age Range Primary (3-5).

Social Skill Objectives Turn taking, transitioning, cooperating with team-mates.

Equipment and Materials Needed A 15-by 15-yard area, cones to define the playing area, soccer ball, pinnies.

PROCEDURE

Divide the class into teams of four. One team starts with the ball and attempts to make five consecutive passes to score a point (see figure 8.4). The team that is not passing the ball tries to intercept the ball from the passing team. If the ball is intercepted, the intercepting team begins trying to make five consecutive passes. If that team loses possession, the other team attempts to make five passes.

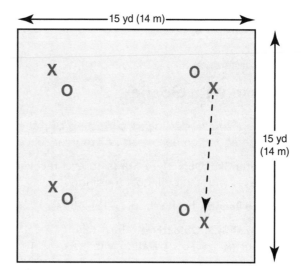

FIGURE 8.4 Setup for 4v4 Passing soccer game.

HELPFUL HINTS AND MODIFICATIONS

- Modify the number of consecutive passes to accommodate the skill level of the teams.
- Provide different sizes and types of balls.

Based on Mitchell, Oslin, and Griffin 2006.

3v3 (no goalie)

In this activity, students pass and receive in a 20- by 20-yard area.

Motor Skill Objectives Passing and receiving, off-the-ball movement.

Age Range Middle school (6-8).

Social Skill Objectives Turn taking, transitioning, cooperating with teammates.

Equipment and Materials Needed (note space requirements) 20- by 20-yard area, soccer ball, pinnies, cones for goals.

PROCEDURE

Divide the class into teams of three. Teams must make five consecutive passes before they can shoot on goal. If the ball is intercepted, the opposing team becomes the attack. The defending team can try to stop the other team from scoring a goal. If the defending team gets the ball, that team immediately starts trying to complete five passes before getting down to their goal to shoot. If a goal is scored, the defending team starts with a throw-in from the goal line, passing begins, and that team becomes the attack team.

HELPFUL HINTS AND MODIFICATIONS

- Assign a peer coach to assist with off-the-ball movement.
- Vary the number of passes required before shooting.

Based on Mitchell, Oslin, and Griffin 2006.

Soccer—High School

4v4 Game With Goalie

This is a small-sided game consisting of three field players and a goalie (two attackers and one defender) on each team. All regular soccer rules apply.

Motor Skill Objectives Passing and receiving, off-the-ball movement, support for the player with the ball, goal tending.

Age Range High school (9-12), 18+.

Social Skill Objectives Turn taking, transitioning, cooperating with teammates.

Equipment and Materials Needed (note space requirement) 40- by 40-yard play area, two goals, soccer ball, pinnies, cones to designated goalie area and game boundaries.

PROCEDURE

This is a small-sided game that follows regulation soccer rules. Divide the class into teams of four with two attackers, one defender, and one goalie (figure 8.5). Attack tries to bring the ball down the field and score a goal. When a goal is scored, the goalie kicks or throws the ball into play for a restart.

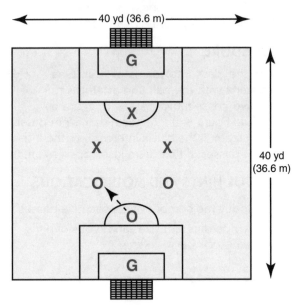

FIGURE 8.5 4v4 Game With Goalie.

HELPFUL HINTS AND MODIFICATIONS

- Plan ahead by creating teams.
- Vary the size of the team or the play area (or both).
- Don't keep score; let students play for fun.

Based on Mitchell, Oslin, and Griffin 2006.

Team Handball—Primary

4v4 Passing Team Handball

This is a small-sided team handball game (two attackers, one defender, and one goalie). Students work on completing five consecutive passes before shooting on goal.

Motor Skill Objectives Throwing and catching, off-the-ball movement.

Age Range Primary (3-5).

Social Skill Objectives Turn taking, transitioning, cooperating with teammates.

Equipment and Materials Needed   Half a gym area, 8-inch (20 cm) ball, pinnies, floor tape or Hot Spots to mark the goal area, goal.

PROCEDURE

Divide the class into teams of four. Games start with a jump ball in the middle of the court, and teams must make five consecutive passes before shooting on goal. Players are not allowed to run with the ball and must throw the ball to a teammate to move it down the court. Players are not allowed to hold on to the ball for more than three seconds. Only one defender may guard the person with the ball. No physical contact is allowed (players must stay an arm's distance from players they are defending), and players may not strip the ball. The ball may only be intercepted on a pass. If the ball is fumbled and touches the floor, the other team gets the ball. Only the goalie is allowed inside the goalie box. After a goal, the goalie throws the ball into play.

HELPFUL HINTS AND MODIFICATIONS

- Assign a peer coach to assist with off-the-ball movement and directed passing.
- Vary the size and type of balls.
- Change the number of consecutive passes based on the skill level of the teams.

Team Handball—Middle School

4v4 Modified Handball

In this game, teammates pass a ball to each other and move down the court. They then try to throw the ball into the other team's goal.

Motor Skill Objectives   Throwing and catching, dribbling with the hands under pressure and shooting on goal, off-the-ball movement.

Age Range   Middle school (6-8).

Social Skill Objectives   Turn taking, transitioning, cooperating with teammates.

Equipment and Materials Needed   Half a gym area, two goals, floor tape or Hot Spots to create a goal area, 6-inch (15 cm) gator skin ball (or ball of similar size), pinnies.

Students playing a game of Modified Handball.

PROCEDURE

Divide the class into teams of four. Play begins with a jump ball. The attack may move with the ball by dribbling no more than three times before passing or shooting on goal. Defenders must be an arm's distance from attack players, and only one defender can mark one attack player. Only the goalie may be inside the goal area. When a goal is scored, the goalie throws it into play. If the attack fumbles the ball and it touches the ground, the opposing team gets the ball.

HELPFUL HINTS AND MODIFICATIONS

- Use different sizes and types of balls.
- Assign a peer coach to help with off-the-ball movement.
- Change team sizes (e.g., to 3v3) depending on the skill level of the players.
- Have students play games of two to three minutes, and rotate teams in and out.

Team Handball—High School

7v7 Modified Handball

In this game, players move the ball down the court by passing a ball to each other. They then try to throw the ball into the other team's goal.

Motor Skill Objectives Throwing and catching, shooting on goal, dribbling with the hands under pressure, off-the-ball movement.

Age Range High school (9-12), 18+.

Social Skill Objectives Turn taking, transitioning, cooperating with teammates.

Equipment and Materials Needed Full gym, two goals, pinnies, floor tape or Hot Spots to denote goalie area, 6-inch (15 cm) super safe ball.

PROCEDURE

Divide the class into teams of seven with positions that include a left wing, circle runner (center), right wing, left backcourt, right backcourt, center backcourt, and goalie (see figure 8.6). Each team attempts to pass or dribble the ball down the court. Players are allowed to dribble the ball for an unlimited amount of time, run with the ball for up to three steps before and after dribbling, and hold the ball without moving for up to three seconds. Any breaking of the rules results in a turnover to the other team. Players are not allowed to endanger an opponent with the ball; pull, hit, or punch the ball out of the hands of an opponent; or contact the ball below the knees. After a point is scored, the goalie throws the ball back in play. Only the goalie is allowed inside the goal area.

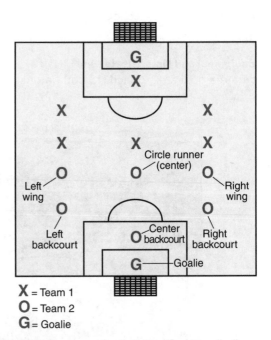

FIGURE 8.6 Setup for 7v7 Modified Handball game.

HELPFUL HINTS AND MODIFICATIONS

- Change the game to 3v3 or 5v5 to encourage more touches of the ball.
- Assign a peer coach to assist students with off-the-ball movement or passing and receiving.
- Vary the size of the playing field.
- Use additional players as sideline players.

Volleyball—Primary
Zone Newcomb

This is a 6v6 catching volleyball game—a small-sided game in which the players catch the ball and toss it two more times on their side of the net or toss it over the net to the opponent's side.

Motor Skill Objectives   Throwing and catching, performing the correct cues for the underhand serve.

Age Range   Primary (3-5).

Social Skill Objectives   Turn taking, transitioning, cooperating with teammates.

Equipment and Materials Needed   Half a volleyball court, volleyball net, trainer or regulation volleyball.

PROCEDURE

Divide the playing area on each side of the net into six boxes. Each player is assigned a box. Having a defined area to play in works well for younger students. Service begins with an underhand serve or toss over the net to the opposing team, whose players attempt to catch the ball and toss it back over the net. A rear zone player who catches the ball can choose to pass it to a player in one of the front zones. Players may pass the ball twice before they have to toss it over the net. If the ball touches the ground or is not caught on the serve, the serving team gets a point. The server continues to serve until the team loses the point. If the ball is passed over the net after the serve and drops, the opposing team gets a point and then serves. Players rotate positions when changing servers.

HELPFUL HINTS AND MODIFICATIONS

- Plan ahead by creating teams.
- Vary the size of the team or the play area (or both).
- Have a variety of sizes and types of balls to make use of the challenge by choice model (in which students choose the equipment they are comfortable with).
- Vary the net height.
- Assign a peer coach.

3v3 Volleyball

In this game, players have more of an opportunity to make contact with the volleyball compared to a traditional volleyball game.

Motor Skill Objectives   Underhand volleyball serve, overhead volleyball pass.

Age Range   Middle school (6-8).

Social Skill Objectives   Turn taking, transitioning, cooperating with teammates, team tactics, positioning.

Equipment and Materials Needed   Half a volleyball court (lengthwise), trainer or regulation volleyball, volleyball net.

PROCEDURE

Create teams of three players, with two players up front and one player in the back (server) (figure 8.7). Team A serves the ball from anywhere on the court. Team B is ready to receive the serve. Players must hit the ball a minimum of two times before returning it over the net. Regulation scoring rules apply.

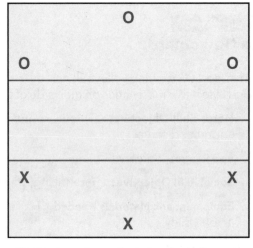

FIGURE 8.7   Setup for 3v3 Volleyball game.

HELPFUL HINTS AND MODIFICATIONS

- Plan ahead by creating teams.
- Offer serving choices (e.g., servers may stand where they choose when serving, or they may select the type of serve to use).
- Vary the size of the team or the play area (or both).
- Have a variety of types and sizes of balls to make use of the challenge by choice model.
- Vary the net height.
- Assign a peer coach.

6v6 Volleyball

This activity is a regulation volleyball game.

Motor Skill Objectives   Overhand or underhand serving using cues, passing, setting.

Age Range   High school (9-12), 18+.

Social Skill Objectives   Turn taking, transitioning, cooperation, communication skills.

Equipment and Materials Needed   Regulation size volleyball court, regulation height net, volleyball.

PROCEDURE

Create teams of six with three front and three back positions. Teams volley for serve. The serving team begins the game with an underhand or overhead serve. The receiving team passes and sets the ball to get it over the net. Encourage multiple hits and setups. Regulation rules apply with standard rotation on the serve.

HELPFUL HINTS AND MODIFICATIONS

- Plan ahead by creating teams.
- Offer serving choices.
- Vary the size of the team or the play area (or both).
- Have a variety of balls sizes.
- Vary the net height.
- Allow the server to serve from anywhere inside her court.

References

Preface

Autism speaks. (n.d.). Retrieved from www.autism-speaks.org/?utm_source=autismspeaks.org&utm_medium=web&utm_campaign=primarymenu.

Fisher, M., & Meyer, L.H. (2002). Development and social competence after two years for students enrolled in inclusive and self-contained education programs. *Research and Practice for Persons with Severe Disabilities, 27,* 165-174.

Goodman, G., & Williams, C. (2007). Interventions for increasing the academic engagement of students with autism spectrum disorders in inclusive classrooms. *Teaching Exceptional Children, 39* (6), 53-61.

Individuals with Disabilities Education Act, 20 U.S.C. §§ 1400 *et seq.* (2004).

Schreibman, L. (2005). *The science and fiction of autism.* Cambridge, MA: Harvard University Press.

Chapter 1

American Association for Physical Activity and Recreation. (2010). Eligibility criteria for adapted physical education services. Reston, VA: Author.

American Psychiatric Association (APA). (2000). *Diagnostic and statistical manual of mental disorders: Text revision* (4th ed.). Washington, DC: Author.

Biklen, D. (2000). Constructing inclusion: Lessons from critical, disability narratives. *International Journal of Inclusive Education, 4,* 337-353.

Block, M.E. (2007). *A teacher's guide to including children with disabilities in general physical education* (3rd ed.). Baltimore, MD: Paul H. Brookes.

Block, M., & Obrusnikova, I. (2007). Inclusion in physical education: A review of the literature from 1995-2005. *Adapted Physical Activity Quarterly, 24* (2), 103-124.

Centers for Disease Control and Prevention. (2009, October 5). CDC statement on ASD data. Retrieved from www.cdc.gov/ncbddd/ASD/facts.html.

Davis, L.J. (1997). *Constructing normalcy. The disabilities studies reader.* New York: Routledge.

Grenier, M. (2007). Inclusion in physical education: From the medical model to social constructionism. *Quest, 59* (3), 298-310.

Horvat, M., Kalakian, L., Croce, R., & Dahlstrom, V. (2011). *Developmental/adapted physical education: Making ability count* (5th ed.). Boston: Benjamin Cummings.

Individuals with Disabilities Education Act, 20 U.S.C. §§ 1400 *et seq.* (2004).

Kluth, P. (2010). *"You're going to love this kid!" Teaching students with ASD in the inclusive classroom* (2nd ed.). Baltimore, MD: Paul H. Brookes.

Merges, J. (2011). *Social enjoyment groups for children, teens and young adults with autism spectrum disorders.* London: Jessica Kingsley.

Pan, C.Y., Tsai, C.L., & Hsieh, K.W. (2011). Physical activity correlates for children with ASD spectrum disorders in middle school physical education. *Research Quarterly for Exercise and Sport, 82* (3), 491-498.

Sherrill, C. (2004). *Adapted physical activity, recreation, and sport: Crossdisciplinary and lifespan* (6th ed.). New York: McGraw-Hill.

Tripp, A., & Rizzo, T. (2006). Disability labels affect physical educators. *Adapted Physical Activity Quarterly, 23,* 310-326.

U.S. Department of Education. (2009). 28th annual report to Congress on the implementation of the Individuals with Disabilities Education Act, 2006. Washington, DC: Author.

Chapter 2

Baker, B., Blacher, J., Crnic, K., & Edelbrook, C. (2002). Behavior problems and parenting stress in families of three-year old children with and without developmental delays. *American Journal of Mental Retardation, 107,* 433-444

Baker-Ericzen, M., Brookman-Frazee, L., & Stahmer, A. (2005). Stress levels and adaptability in parents of toddlers with and without autism spectrum disorder. *Research & Practice for Persons with Severe Disabilities, 30,* 194-204.

Dawson, G., & Rosonoff, M. (n.d.). Sports, exercise, and the benefits of physical activity for individuals with autism. Retrieved from www.autismspeaks.org/science/science-news/sports-exercise-and-benefits-physical.

Kozub, F.M. (2008). Goal-directed physical education for learners with disabilities. *Palaestra, 24* (2), 19-27.

Meadan, H., Halle, J., & Ebata, A. (2010). Families with children who have autism spectrum disorders: Stress and support. *Exceptional Children, 77,* 7-36.

Pottie, C.G., & Ingram, K.M. (2008). Daily stress, coping, and well-being in parents of children with autism: A multilevel modeling approach. *Journal of Family Psychology*, 22, 855-864.

Smith, L.E., Hong, J., Seltzer, M.M., Greenberg, J.S., Almeida, D.M., & Bishop, S.L. (2010). Daily experiences among mothers of adolescents and adults with autism spectrum disorder. *Journal of Autism and Developmental Disorders*, 40, 167-178.

Chapter 3

Black, K., & Williamson, D. (2011). Designing inclusive physical activity games. In A. Cereijo Roibas, W. Stamatakis, & K. Black (Eds.), *Design for sport.* Surrey, UK: Gower.

Block, M.E. (2007). *A teacher's guide to including children with disabilities in general physical education* (3rd ed.). Baltimore, MD: Paul H. Brookes.

Broderick, A., Mehta-Parekh, H., & Reid, D.K. (2005). Differentiating instruction for disabled students in inclusive classrooms. *Theory into Practice, 44,* 194-202.

Cereijo Roibas, A., Stamatakis, W., & Black, K. (Eds.). (2011). *Design for sport.* Surrey, UK: Gower.

Davis, R. (2011). *Teaching disability sport: A guide for physical educators.* Champaign, IL: Human Kinetics.

Ellis, K., Lieberman, L., & LeRoux, D. (2009). Using differentiated instruction in physical education. *Palaestra, 24* (4), 19-23.

Graham, G., Holt/Hale, S., & Parker, M. (2009). *Children moving: Reflective approach to teaching physical education* (7th ed.). Mt. View, CA: Mayfield.

Grenier, M., & Yeaton, P. (2011). Previewing: A successful strategy for students with autism. *Journal of Physical Education, Recreation & Dance, 82* (1), 28-33.

Johnson, D., & Johnson, R. (1991). *Learning together and alone* (3rd ed.). Englewood Cliffs, NJ: Prentice Hall.

Mosston, M., & Ashworth, S. (2002). *Teaching physical education* (5th ed.). Boston: Benjamin Cummings.

Sherrill, C. (2004). *Adapted physical activity, recreation, and sport: Crossdisciplinary and lifespan* (6th ed.). New York: McGraw-Hill.

Stevenson, P. (2009). The pedagogy of inclusive youth sport. In H. Fitzgerald (Ed.), *Disability and youth sport* (pp. 119-131). London: Routledge.

Winnick, J.P. (Ed.). (2011). *Adapted physical education and sport* (5th ed.). Champaign, IL: Human Kinetics.

Chapter 4

Banda, D., Copple, K., Koul, R., Sancibrian, S., & Bogschutz, R. (2010). Video modelling interventions to teach spontaneous requesting using AAC devices to individuals with autism: A preliminary investigation. *Disability and Rehabilitation, 32* (16), 1364-1372.

Charlop-Christy, M.H., & Daneshvar, S. (2003). Using video modeling to teach perspective taking to children with autism. *Journal of Positive Behavior Interventions, 5* (1), 12-21.

Donnellan, A., Leary, M., & Robledo, J. (2009). Stress and coping in autism. In L. Eckenrode, P. Fennell, K. Hearsey, & B. Reynolds (Eds.), *Tasks galore: Let's play.* Raleigh, NC: Tasks Galore.

Fittipaldi-Wert, J., & Mowling, C. (2009). Using visual supports for students with autism in physical education. *Journal of Physical Education, Recreation & Dance, 80* (2), 39-43.

Gray, C. (2000). *The new social story book.* Arlington, TX: Future Horizons.

Grenier, M., & Yeaton, P. (2011). Previewing: A successful strategy for students with autism. *Journal of Physical Education, Recreation & Dance, 82* (1), 28-33.

Loovis, M. (2011). Behavior management. In J. Winnick (Ed.), *Adapted physical education and sport* (5th ed., pp. 101-118). Champaign, IL: Human Kinetics.

Mesibov, G.B., Shea, V., & Schopler, E. (2004). *The TEACCH approach to autism spectrum disorders.* New York: Springer.

Rayner, C., Denholm, C., & Sigafoos, J. (2009). Video-based intervention for individuals with autism: Key questions that remain unanswered. *Research in Autism Spectrum Disorders, 3,* 291-303.

Wallin, J. (2009). *Teaching children with autism: A resource.* Retrieved from www.polyxo.com.

Waugh, L., Bowers, T., & French, R. (2007). Use of picture cards in integrated physical education classes. *Strategies, 20* (4), 18-20.

Chapter 5

Cheung, P., & Siu, A. (2009). A comparison of patterns of sensory processing in children with and without developmental disabilities. *Research in Developmental Disabilities, 30,* 1468-1480.

Corbett, B.A., Mendoza, S., Abdullah, M., Wegelin, J.A., & Levine, S. (2006). Cortisol circadian rhythms and response to stress in children with ASD. *Psychoneuroendocrinology, 31,* 59-68.

Crane, L., Goddard, L., & Pring, L. (2009). Sensory processing in adults with ASD spectrum disorders. *Autism, 13* (3), 215-228.

Haywood, K.M., & Getchell, N. (2009). *Life span motor development* (5th ed.). Champaign, IL: Human Kinetics.

Jansen, L.M., Gispen-de Wied, C.C., Jansen, M.A., van der Gaag, R.J., Mattbys, W., & van Engeland, H. (1999).

Pituitary-adrenal reactivity in a child psychiatric population: Salivary cortisol response to stressors. *European Neuropsychopharmacology, 9,* 67-75.

Jasmin, E., Couture, M., McKinley, P., Reid, G., Fombonne, E., & Gisel, E. (2009). Sensori-motor and daily living skills of preschool children with ASD spectrum disorder. *Journal of ASD and Developmental Disabilities, 39,* 231-241.

Jones, R., Quigney, C., & Huws, J. (2003). First-hand accounts of sensory perceptual experiences in ASD: A qualitative analysis. *Journal of Intellectual & Developmental Disabilities, 28* (2), 112-121.

Lee, L.C., Harrington, R.A., Louie, B.B., & Newschaffer, C.J. (2008). Children with ASD: Quality of life and parental concerns. *Journal of Autism and Developmental Disorder, 38,* 1147-1160.

Lytle, R., & Todd, T. (2009). Stress and the student with ASD spectrum disorder. *Teaching Exceptional Children, 41* (4), 36-42.

Tani, P., Lindberg, N., Matto, V., Appelberg, B., Nieminen-von Wendt, T., von Wendt, L., et al. (2005). Higher plasma AGTH levels in adults with Asperger syndrome. *Journal of Psychosomatic Research, 58,* 533-536.

Chapter 6

Block, M.E., Lieberman, L.J., & Connor-Kuntz, F. (1998). Authentic assessment in adapted physical education. *The Journal of Physical Education, Recreation, & Dance, 69* (3), 48-55.

Bruninks, R.H., & Bruninks, B.D. (2005). *Bruininks-Oseretsky test of motor proficiency* (2nd ed.). San Antonio, TX: Pearson.

D'Ateno, P., Mangiapanello, K., & Taylor, B.A. (2003). Using video modeling to teach complex play sequences to a preschooler with autism. *Journal of Positive Behavior Interventions, 5* (1), 5-11.

Delano, M.E. (2007). Video modeling interventions for individuals with autism. *Remedial & Special Education, 28* (1), 33-42.

Folio, M.R., & Fewell, R.R. (2000). *Peabody developmental motor scales* (2nd ed.). Austin, TX: PRO-ED.

Henderson, S.E., & Sugden, D.A. (2007). *Movement assessment battery for children (Movement ABC-2)* (2nd ed.). San Antonio, TX: Pearson.

Hine, J.F., & Wolery, M. (2006). Using point-of-view video modeling to teach play to preschoolers with autism. *Topics in Early Childhood Special Education, 26* (2), 83-93.

Horvat, M., Block, M.E., & Kelly, L.E. (2007). *Developmental and adapted physical activity assessment.* Champaign, IL: Human Kinetics.

Meredith, M., & Welk, G.J. (Eds.). (2010). *Fitnessgram and activitygram: Test administration manual* (4th ed.). Champaign, IL: Human Kinetics.

Payne, V.G., Yan, J.H., & Block, M.E. (2010). *Human motor development in individuals with and without disabilities.* New York: Nova Science.

Sandt, D. (2008). Social stories for students with autism in physical education. *Journal of Physical Education, Recreation, and Dance, 79* (6), 42-45.

Savner, J.L., & Myles, B.S. (2000). *Making visual supports work in the home and community.* Shawnee Mission, KS: Autism Asperger Publishing.

Siedentop, D. (1994). *Sport education: Quality PE through positive sport experiences.* Champaign, IL: Human Kinetics.

Silliman-French, L., Buswell, D.J., & French, R. (2008). *Statewide physical fitness testing and students with disabilities in Texas.* Retrieved from www.tahperd.org/LINKS/links_pdfs/Fitness_Testing_Special_Needs.pdf.

Special Olympics. (2011). *Special Olympics tennis guide.* Retrieved from www.specialolympics.org/tennis.aspx.

Ulrich, D.A. (2000). *Test of gross motor development (TGMD-2)* (2nd ed.). Austin, TX: PRO-ED.

Winnick, J., & Short, F. (1999). *The Brockport physical fitness test manual.* Champaign, IL: Human Kinetics.

Chapter 8

Clumpner, R. (2003). *Sport progressions.* Champaign, IL: Human Kinetics.

Dowson, A. (2009). *More fun and games: 100 new sport-related activities.* Champaign, IL: Human Kinetics.

Mitchell, S.A., Oslin, J.L., & Griffin, L.L. (2006). *Teaching sport concepts and skills: A tactical games approach* (2nd ed.). Champaign, IL: Human Kinetics.

National Association for Sport and Physical Education (NASPE). (2004). *Moving into the future: National standards for physical education: A guide to content and assessment* (2nd ed.). Reston, VA: Author.

Index

Note: The italicized *f* and *t* following page numbers refer to figures and tables, respectively.

About the Editor

Michelle Grenier, PhD, is an associate professor and coordinator of the physical education and adapted physical education program at the University of New Hampshire in Durham. She has substantial experience in researching, teaching, and presenting on inclusion and autism spectrum disorders. Dr. Grenier has taught at the elementary, middle, and high school levels and worked with students with disabilities in general and adapted physical education settings. She has presented at the state, national, and international levels and is currently the adapted physical education representative for the New Hampshire Association of Health, Physical Education, Recreation and Dance. Dr. Grenier also served as chair of the Adapted Physical Education Council for AAPAR and AAHPERD.

About the Contributors

Martin Block, PhD, is a professor in the kinesiology program at the University of Virginia. He is best known for his research on including students with disabilities in general physical education as well as his consulting work with Special Olympics, Inc. He has been the director of the master's program in adapted physical education (APE) at the University of Virginia since 1993. He has authored or coauthored six books and more than 75 refereed articles. Block is also the former president of the National Consortium for Physical Education for Individuals with Disabilities (NCPEID).

Ann Griffin, MA, is an adapted physical education consultant and member of the autism team at Grant Wood Area Education Agency in Cedar Rapids, Iowa. She assists physical educators in 33 districts in adapting and developing curriculum, instruction, equipment, and assessment for students with disabilities. Griffin has worked as an itinerant adapted physical education teacher, consultant, and adjunct instructor. She was selected as the National Adapted Physical Education Teacher of the Year in 2005 and has presented at state, national, and international conferences. She is especially fond of *unique* students and interesting brains. Her particular areas of interest and expertise include teaching students with autism spectrum disorders and equipment innovation.

Rebecca K. Lytle, PhD, is a professor in the department of kinesiology at California State University at Chico, where she teaches courses in adapted physical education and motor development. Lytle has been teaching in higher education since 1992. She also taught as an adapted physical education teacher in the public schools from 1988 to 1996, and was a school consultant from 2000 to 2002. Lytle has published numerous articles for refereed journals and coauthored three books and six book chapters on adapted physical activity. She has presented at the state, national, and international levels and has served as consultant or coordinator for several community-based physical activity and motor skill assessment programs for both children and adults. She served as chair of the National Adapted Physical Activity Council of AAHPERD and chair of the California State Council on Adapted Physical Education.

Andrea Taliaferro, PhD, is an assistant professor in the college of physical activity and sport sciences at West Virginia University. She is best known for her work on investigating self-efficacy of physical educators who work with children with disabilities, and for her work on enhancing community-based recreational opportunities for individuals with disabilities. Dr. Taliaferro was an adapted physical education specialist in public schools for seven years and also has teaching experience as a general physical educator. She has published refereed articles and has presented at state, national, and international conferences. She is a certified adapted physical educator through the National Consortium for Physical Education for Individuals with Disabilities (NCPEID), and has served as a representative on the West Virginia AHPERD board as an at-large board member for NCPEID.

Teri Todd, PhD, is an assistant professor and director of clinical operations in the Center of Achievement at California State University, Northridge. She has many years of experience with people with autism spectrum disorders (ASD) as a parent, teacher, and researcher. Dr. Todd is particularly interested in exploring methods to engage individuals with ASD in sustained physical activity, as well as best practices in preparing preservice special education teachers to work with children on the spectrum. She has presented research and workshops at state, national, and international conferences. Dr. Todd served as the president-elect of the California State Council for Exceptional Children (CEC) Division on Autism and Developmental Disabilities (DADD) chapter.

Pat Yeaton, MEd, is a physical education teacher at North Hampton School in North Hampton, New Hampshire. She is also an adjunct professor at the University of New Hampshire in Durham. Yeaton has taught at the elementary and middle school levels for 25 years and uses the full inclusion model as her physical education teaching model. She has presented on inclusion and autism spectrum disorders at local, state, and national conferences. Yeaton is currently the vertical team leader for physical education in School Administrative Unit 21. She was also the New Hampshire Elementary Physical Education Teacher of the Year in 2005.